Praise for Ring of Wisdom

I have always loved listening to a good story and it is a privilege to listen to true stories from the life of a woman who has so much wisdom to offer. Sit down with a cup of tea or a glass of wine and savor the stories and lessons Sandy Bonney offers in her beautiful book. They will give you time to pause, reflect and decide what's next for you.

—Susan Scott, New York Times bestselling author of *Fierce Love, Fierce Conversations* & *Fierce Leadership* and the founder of Fierce, Inc.

In *The Ring of Wisdom*, Sandy Bonney has given us a gift that, when opened, reveals to us our true depth. It entices us to wander down the path of self-discovery considering new parts of ourselves we may have previously diminished or disregarded. As you explore, you may well discover that you have more wisdom, boldness, and resilience than you expected.

—Dan Newby, Author of *The Unopened Gift* and co-founder of Dignity Inc.

The Ring of Wisdom reminds us of something often overlooked—wisdom doesn't come from thinking more, but from feeling more honestly. Sandy shows that emotions aren't distractions; they are the pathway to wisdom, growth, and dignity. Anyone serious about living intentionally and leading authentically will find something meaningful here.

—Marcel Brunel, co-founder of Dignity Inc.
and Author of *Dignity in Policing*

Sandy Bonney's book is a beautifully written invitation to pause, reflect, and reconnect with the wisdom within. She has a remarkable way of turning life's experiences—both joyful and challenging—into meaningful insight that speaks directly to the heart.

What makes this book so powerful is not just what she teaches, but how she lives it. Her authenticity, courage, and commitment to growth shine through every page. This is more than a book you read—it's one you experience, revisit, and carry with you.

A truly inspiring guide for anyone ready to grow, heal, and step more fully into the life they're meant to live.

—Stacie Leverette, Executive Leadership Coach, KW-MAPS Coaching

In this book, Sandy Bonney models authenticity and vulnerability, inviting readers into deeper self-awareness, where true transformation begins and unfolds.

—Alaine Sonnenberg, Author of *Emotions Empower*

The Ring of Wisdom offers a thoughtful blueprint for self-reflection. In a fast-paced world full of distractions, Sandy's raw and deeply personal stories help readers slow down and reconnect with themselves in a deeply human way.

—Liz Lents, Journalist and Fox News Producer

A thoughtful reflection that inspires you to believe that something more is possible. It encourages you to ask brave questions of yourself, using the quiet strength within. A timely and timeless truth on how to rewrite your story, navigating life's challenges, in order to find lasting peace in a changing world.

—Ron Fredette

The Ring of Wisdom is one of those rare books that feel less like something you read and more like something you live inside of. Sandy Bonney has done something beautifully brave here. She has opened her life, her losses, her lessons, and her faith, and laid them down like a warm fire for the rest of us to gather around.

This is not a book that tells you what to do. It is a book that reminds you of who you already are. I found myself underlining, pausing, praying, and exhaling all the way through.

Every woman I know needs this book on her nightstand. The ones who are thriving, the ones who are healing, and especially the ones who are still trying to find their way back to themselves. Sandy Bonney has written something that will outlast her and that, beloved, is legacy.

—Shakara Campbell, Associate Broker at Keller Williams Realty

The Ring of Wisdom is a beautiful and heartfelt invitation to the reader to pause, reflect, heal, and grow. Sandy Bonney writes in a style that brings warmth, grace, and honesty. She guides the reader through the very places life shapes us. These pages feel personal, wise, and deeply moving. This is the kind of book that meets a woman where she is and helps her move forward with greater understanding, peace, and strength.

—Dianna Kokoszka, Author, international speaker, entrepreneur and former CEO of Keller Williams Realty International MAPS Coaching and Training

The Ring Of Wisdom

How Love, Loss and Life Shape the Woman You're Becoming

Sandy Bonney

Printed and bound in the United States of America
Interior illustrations by Cheyenne Bonney

ISBNs:
Paperback: 979-8-9955040-0-9
Hardback: 979-8-9955040-1-6
Ebook: 979-8-9955040-2-3

Begin the Journey with Me

THIS BOOK WAS WRITTEN AS AN INVITATION—AN INVITATION TO PAUSE, reflect, and rediscover the wisdom already living within you. My hope is that as you read, you will feel wrapped in warmth, reflection, and love.

If you would like to continue exploring these ideas beyond the pages of this book, I invite you to join the Ring of Wisdom community.

When you subscribe at www.theringofwisdom.com, you'll receive updates, my monthly newsletter, and invitations to future gatherings, retreats, and special events designed to support your emotional and personal growth.

Wisdom is not something that we arrive at once.

It is something we return to—again and again—throughout our lives.

I would be honored to continue this journey with you.

With gratitude,

Sandy Bonney

Blessed is the one who finds wisdom,
and the one who gets understanding,
for the gain from her is better
than gain from silver
and her profit better than gold.
She is more precious than jewels,
and nothing you desire can compare with her.
Long life is in her right hand;
in her left hand are riches and honor.
Her ways are ways of pleasantness,
and all her paths are peace.
She is a tree of life to those who lay hold of her;
those who hold her fast are called blessed.

Proverbs 3:13–18

Dedication

To my grandmothers, Helena Woehrle and Flora Lindsley. I love and miss you both dearly. Your strength, steadiness, and unwavering love taught me what it truly means to care for family and others.

Contents

Preface

Welcome.

Did you think you would be more successful by now? You've been desiring this life, but something keeps you from living it. Do you believe you were created for something more? If so, you are not alone. I stood behind a salon chair for twenty years enjoying conversation after conversation. Stories that created experiences of wisdom and growth. As a leader, mother, and grandmother, I have my own stories—some of which didn't serve me, so I needed to examine what I was telling people, mostly myself.

I understand the importance of the work that is involved in reaching our full potential. I'm still on this path of growth. I remember my grandmother saying that growth is optional in life.

The last twenty years as a coach and business owner, I have had the honor of learning, meeting, loving, and growing from so many. I have been able to study the motivation of highly successful people and help support them.

The title *The Ring of Wisdom* was born from summers of my childhood, when my family gathered around a campfire. As children, we sat quietly, sometimes on logs, sometimes on cool grass, surrounded by generations of wisdom. Parents, grandparents, aunts, uncles, cousins, and neighbors formed a loose circle around the fire, sharing stories that felt bigger than time itself.

I listened with fascination.

I remember wondering if I would ever be that wise...or that talented. My Uncle George played the guitar and the harmonica. His songs were filled with stories of the "good old days"—how life was lived, loved, and learned. The adults seemed peaceful. Grounded. Present. Even we children felt it. As I looked around the circle, each face held a different glow, cast by the same fire.

To this day, regardless of what is happening in my life or around me, a fire burning in front of me brings me into stillness. Whether it's the fireplace at our cottage, the firepit at our mainland home, or even a gas flame, my body relaxes and my breath slows.

There is something about a fire's steady burn—its warmth, rhythm, and shifting colors. It feels almost hypnotic, as if time folds in on itself. Past, present, and future seem to sit together. Some of the most meaningful moments of my life have unfolded around a ring of fire—stories overlapping with laughter, old experiences shared, softened, and sometimes finally released.

Wisdom is passed without instruction—simply by being shared.

That is where *The Ring of Wisdom* began.

Wisdom, I've come to understand, is not a straight line. It is not something we achieve once and move beyond. Wisdom is a circle. Each experience, each lesson, each season of life brings us back to ourselves—deeper, steadier, and more whole than before.

Every chapter in this book represents a place on that ring—formed by experience, habits, reflection, emotion, and choice. Some wisdoms arrive early in life. Others come through struggle, loss, growth, or courage. Many return us to lessons we thought we already knew, now with greater understanding.

These wisdoms are distinct, yet deeply connected. They overlap and build upon one another. Just like the stories around that campfire, no single voice stands alone. Together, they create something lasting.

This book is an invitation to step into that circle with me—to reflect, to listen, and to notice where wisdom has already been forming in your own life.

Since I was a little girl, I've believed that someday I would be changing lives and living my best life. The journey to that dream required living fully, learning deeply, and embracing the lessons along the way. By sharing my personal stories with you, my hope is that your own path may feel a little lighter, more honored, and more possible.

It is never too late to say, *Why not me?*

Your dreams are worthy of being lived—with passion, courage, and love.

Before you turn the final page, take a moment and ask yourself:

What wisdom is already forming in my life?

If the stories and reflections in this book help even one person step into their boldness and begin living the life they were meant for, then writing this book will have been more than worth it.

Hugs,

Sandy

A Map for Our Journeys

Before we begin our first journey, I want to offer a gentle invitation on how to move through this book. There is no single path around the ring—only the one that feels right for you.

This book is not meant to be rushed.

It is meant to be *entered*.

Each chapter is a journey—a ring of lessons. Together, these rings form wisdom that shapes who we are becoming and the life we are choosing to live.

Some journeys may feel familiar. Others may feel tender. A few may surprise you.

You do not need to read this book from beginning to end.

Like sitting around a fire, feeling the warmth. The coziness. The generosity of wisdom given.

Sometimes we lean in, drawn by warmth or curiosity.

Other times we sit quietly, listening, letting the light do its work.

There is no urgency here—only presence.

You may feel drawn to:

- **Self-Care** when you are tired
- **Money** when you are uncertain
- **Family** or **Divorce** when you are grieving or redefining
- **Community** or **Spirituality** when you are longing for belonging
- **Boldness** or **Courage** when you are ready to rise

Let your curiosity guide you.

Let your emotions guide you.

Let your dignity guide you.

If a chapter feels heavy, pause.

If a chapter feels affirming, linger.

If a chapter feels confronting, be gentle with yourself.

There is no "right" way to read this book—only an honest one.

Each journey stands on its own.

Together, they form a ring—one that honors where you've been, where you are, and where you may be going next.

Take what resonates.

Release what doesn't—yet.

Trust that the wisdom you need will meet you at the right time.

And so we begin at the center of the ring—where emotions live. Where experiences become stories, and stories become wisdom.

Emotions are not just something we feel. They are something we integrate and carry forward—a lens through which we see our lives.

Journey One

THE WISDOM OF EMOTIONAL LEARNING

*"When we give ourselves permission to feel,
we give ourselves permission to heal."*
—Unknown

Where Wisdom Begins

EVERY RING OF WISDOM HAS A CENTER.

A place where awareness begins and all other wisdoms are formed.

On the Ring of Wisdom, emotions are not an outer layer—they are the foundation. Before we understand dignity, family, money, leadership, health, or legacy, we must first understand what we feel. Emotions are the gateway through which wisdom speaks.

This first journey begins at the heart of the ring—where self-awareness is born and healing quietly takes root.

My Emotional Learning Journey

Five years ago, I received an invitation that quietly—but profoundly—changed the trajectory of my life: a session on emotional literacy. At the time, I felt lost, hollow, and uncertain about what was next. That invitation arrived like a lifeline, drawing me into a journey I didn't yet have language for—one that would reshape how I understood myself, my relationships, and the world around me.

Learning to engage with my emotions did not happen overnight. It wasn't simply about identifying what I felt; it was about releasing judgment around having those feelings at all. I stopped labeling emotions as "good" or "bad" and began welcoming them as messengers— signals offering insight into my inner world.

Today, when emotions arise, I meet them with curiosity. Sometimes they are clear and immediate; other times, they unfold slowly. I've given myself permission to sit with feelings for hours—or even a full day—without rushing to fix, analyze, or suppress them. In that space, clarity arrives in its own time.

Living in dignity as a way of being, I've learned to ask:

- What emotion am I in?
- Where do I feel it in my body?
- What might this feeling be trying to tell me?

These quiet conversations have taught me patience, presence, and self-compassion. I no longer see emotions as interruptions to manage. I see them as guides—pointing me toward healing, truth, and growth.

As I began listening more closely to my emotions, I also began to wonder where my behavior patterns had come from. Feelings don't appear in isolation—they are shaped over time, often long before we understand them.

The Roots of Emotional Disconnect

Much of my emotional conditioning can be traced back to childhood. My father was emotionally distant and often silent, shaped by trauma he never fully shared. As a child, I didn't understand his lack of expression—only that something always felt missing.

Years later, my grandmother shared a story that brought understanding. My father had polio as a young boy and spent six months hospitalized—far from home, isolated from his family. The physical pain and emotional separation left invisible scars. When he returned, he was changed—quieter, withdrawn, guarded.

That story softened something in me. His silence wasn't rejection—it was survival. This realization opened the door to compassion—not only for him, but for myself.

When emotions are repeatedly unmet or unspoken, they don't disappear. They go quiet. And over time, quiet can feel like strength.

The Cost of Emotional Numbness

For decades, I mistook emotional suppression for strength. In my home, vulnerability was not encouraged. The unspoken rule—children are to be seen and not heard—shaped my sense of worth. I learned early that acceptance came through performance, achievement, and results.

I became skilled at pushing through—driving forward with relentless energy while disconnecting from my inner world. I accomplished a great deal, yet rarely paused to ask why.

Why am I chasing this?

What am I trying to prove?

Only when I slowed down did I recognize how much of my life I had lived from emotional numbness. I had been sprinting toward goals while carrying quiet loneliness and a longing for connection. The dashboard of my life was flashing LOW FUEL, but I kept pressing the gas, convinced momentum alone was enough.

It wasn't.

True success isn't just reaching the finish line—it's being present for the journey. Allowing the heart to participate, not just the mind.

It took time for me to understand that what I had been avoiding was not weakness, but wisdom waiting for permission.

Embracing Emotions as Wisdom

Today, I cherish the drive and determination that once propelled me forward. I no longer see it as something to undo, but as evidence of resilience and perseverance. And now, I invite emotions into that strength.

Emotions are not right or wrong; they simply exist. The more we resist them, the louder they become. When we welcome them, we move forward with balance, understanding, and authenticity.

There are over two hundred identified emotions, yet most of us were taught only a fraction of them. It's been five years, and I've consciously chosen to honor mine every day. What began as personal healing has become a passion and a purpose—helping others reconnect with the wisdom of their emotional lives.

As emotional literacy expands, dignity grows—reducing miscommunication, supporting mental health, and fostering compassion in both personal and professional spaces.

As my relationship with emotions deepened, so did my understanding of wisdom itself. Insight didn't arrive through force or logic—it arrived through feeling.

How Emotions Empower the Ring of Wisdom

Experiences become stories, and stories become wisdom. Through emotion, we create meaning, connection, and a life worth living. Yet when emotions are not acknowledged, those same stories can harden, keeping us stuck in patterns that distance us from our truest selves.

Wisdom does not arrive loudly.

It rarely demands attention.

More often, wisdom whispers—through a feeling, a pause, a moment of discomfort or resonance. It lives in the space between what happens and how we respond. And it is in that space that emotions play their most important role.

Emotions are the carriers of wisdom.

They determine not only what we notice, but how we receive what life is offering us. When we are emotionally open—curious, grounded, present—wisdom has room to land. But when we are overwhelmed, rushed, fearful, or defensive, wisdom often passes us by.

Mood matters more than we realize.

The same experience can teach us something profound one day and leave us unchanged the next—simply because of the emotional lens we are looking through. When we are anxious, we react. When we are calm, we reflect. When we feel threatened, we protect. When we feel safe, we learn.

This is why emotions sit at the center of the Ring of Wisdom. They are the filter through which experience becomes insight—or remains unexamined.

With awareness came curiosity. I wanted to understand not just that emotions mattered, but how they moved beneath the surface.

Understanding Emotions, Moods, and Clusters

Most of us operate with a limited emotional vocabulary. This often leads us to group complex feelings into broad categories to avoid discomfort. Yet emotions are nuanced and frequently appear in clusters—fear with anxiety, doubt with uncertainty, ambition with enthusiasm.

Distinguishing between emotions and moods is equally important. Emotions are typically short-lived responses to events. Moods linger, shaping the emotional backdrop of our days.

When left unresolved, emotional clusters—especially those formed through trauma—can persist and contribute to long-term stress responses. I once lived in recurring clusters of anxiety, fear, and doubt, countering them with ambition and boldness. I believed powering through was the solution.

Healing began when I reframed emotions as signals rather than threats.

There is also a biological reason emotions feel so powerful.

At the center of our emotional experience is the limbic system—the part of the brain responsible for emotion, memory, motivation, and survival responses. It processes experiences quickly and automatically, long before our logical mind has time to catch up.

For years, I have been fascinated by the limbic system and the wisdom built into it. Research shows that mood influences perception, decision-making, motivation, social connection, memory, and attention. When the limbic system senses safety, we are open and reflective. When it senses threat—real or perceived—we become reactive or guarded, or withdrawn.

This means our emotional state doesn't just affect *how we feel*. It affects how we learn, what we remember, and whether wisdom has space to land.

Understanding this helped me soften toward myself. My reactions weren't failures—they were signals. My moods weren't weaknesses—they were information. My emotional patterns weren't flaws—they were adaptive responses shaped over time.

When we begin to work *with* our emotional brain instead of *against* it, awareness replaces judgment. Curiosity replaces fear. And wisdom becomes accessible again.

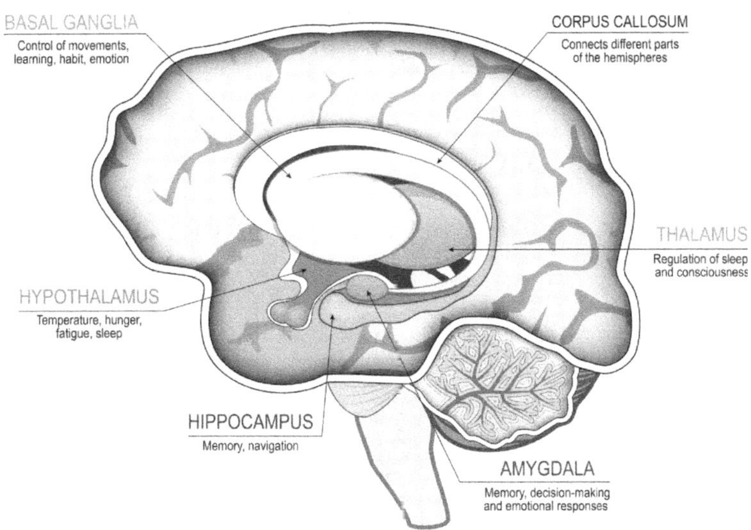

When we understand that emotions are both experiential and biological, we can meet ourselves with greater compassion. Reflection becomes less about fixing and more about noticing.

Wisdom Moment

Emotional learning begins the moment you choose to notice what you feel without judgment.

In that awareness, your emotions shift from reactions into wisdom.

A Pause for Reflection

Take a slow breath in...and gently release it.

Emotional learning is about acknowledgment, nothing to fix or force. Simply notice how we feel.

Emotional Learning—Your Reflective Journey

1. From Judgment to Acceptance

Feels like: Shame, resistance, anticipation

Reveals: Self-compassion

- Which emotion do I judge most quickly in myself?
- What happens when I allow it without fixing it?
- How might kindness change my relationship with this feeling?

2. Achievement Without Presence

Feels like: Numbness, urgency, burnout

Reveals: A longing to be seen and valued

- What have I achieved without fully experiencing it?
- What emotion was I avoiding?
- What might slowing down reveal?

3. Inherited Emotional Patterns

Feels like: Distance, silence, uncertainty

Reveals: Generational survival strategies

- What emotional patterns did I inherit?
- How did they once protect me?
- What new pattern am I choosing?

4. Surrender and Permission

Feels like: Grounding, openness, release

Reveals: Inner wisdom already within

- Where do I feel this emotion in my body?
- What is it asking of me?
- What changes when I allow it fully?

Wisdom to Carry Forward

- Emotions are not problems to solve; they are messages to honor.
- Emotional literacy begins with permission.
- Our past informs our patterns but does not define our future.
- Emotional strength is rooted in connection, not control.
- Pausing to feel is an act of courage.
- The body holds emotional wisdom.

Encouragement for Parents and Leaders

When we learn to meet our own emotions with curiosity instead of control, something shifts. We begin to listen differently—not only to ourselves, but to the people who depend on us.

Leadership is not only about performance or telling people what to do—it is about people and how you care for them. Asking *"What emotion might be present right now?"* can change conversations, relationships, and outcomes. Creating emotionally safe environments builds trust, dignity, and connection.

As the saying goes, *"No one cares how much you know until they know how much you care."*

For parents, emotional literacy offers language, patience, and connection. Parenting is already a roller coaster—learning to understand emotions helps us ride it with less fear and fewer bruises. Over time, it builds trust and strengthens the relationship, modeling healthy emotional habits that children can carry forward into their lives.

A GROUNDING WORD

*"Gracious words are like a honeycomb,
sweetness to the soul and health to the body."*
—Proverbs 16:24

Closing Blessing

The fire in the middle of the ring never changes.
Our emotional distance from it does.
Emotions decide whether wisdom warms us...
or flickers unnoticed in the background.
As you move forward, return often to your breath.
To your body.
To your heart.
You are already enough—exactly as you are.

Journey Two

THE WISDOM OF DIGNITY

"Freedom is the open window through which pours the sunlight of the human spirit and human dignity."
—Herbert Hoover

At the Heart of Dignity

DIGNITY ALLOWS US TO NURTURE AND CARE FOR OURSELVES.

To set and protect our boundaries.

To know—deeply and without condition—I am worthy. I am enough just as I am.

Dignity is the ability to say no when it feels true, not because we are angry, arrogant, or dismissive, but because something simply does not align. It is self-respect without apology. Strength without hardness.

Every Ring of Wisdom has a quality that steadies us when the world feels uncertain.

In this journey, that steadiness is dignity.

Dignity is not something we earn through approval, performance, or compliance. It is something we remember. It lives quietly beneath our roles, titles, and expectations—waiting to be reclaimed.

Dignity leads the way—not by force, but by grounding us in what is true.

This journey explores what happens when dignity steps forward—not as armor, but as grounding truth. Sometimes dignity arrives quietly, not in moments of strength, but in moments of warmth—when we feel safe enough to rest in who we are.

The Coziness of Dignity

Dignity feels like being wrapped in a warm, soft blanket—one that envelops you in love, comfort, and security. It is the quiet reassurance of worth.

For me, dignity arrived unexpectedly on a beautiful summer day.

The sun was shining. The sky was clear. A warm breeze brushed my face as if the world itself were offering affirmation. I had just completed a fulfilling day of coaching and was looking forward to my weekly call with my coach. When the phone rang, I felt a spark of joy—a sense of alignment and purpose.

In that moment, dignity whispered, *You are enough.*

And for the first time, I believed it.

But dignity, like warmth, can be disrupted. And sometimes it is revealed most clearly when it is challenged.

When Dignity Is Tested

As our session began, I sensed a shift. A subtle heaviness moved through the conversation—something unsettled my usually grounded presence.

"Is everything okay?" I asked.

Her response landed like a punch to the gut.

She shared feedback from another coach—someone I barely knew—about my presence during recent Zoom leadership calls. As she spoke, my stomach tightened. Anger, fear, anxiety, and doubt began to swirl. Then came the announcement: I would be contacted by a leadership coach to "discuss it further."

I could feel myself getting upset. I stepped outside, barefoot in the grass, hoping nature could help me process what felt like betrayal. Anger burned, softened into disgust, and settled into disbelief. By the time the call ended, I felt hollow.

Have you ever received a call that leaves you questioning everything?

When dignity is shaken, we often feel it first in the body—before we have words for it.

Dignity Steps In

The call I had been dreading came through about thirty minutes later. I took a deep breath and leaned into the mantra I've relied on in difficult moments: *Listen with love.* Over the years, I've learned that approaching hard conversations with compassion—for myself and for the other person—helps me stay present. It allows me to listen, even when the words are hard to hear.

He opened with commentary about my facial expressions during Zoom calls, suggesting they were affecting others. My first thought was, *What?* As he continued, I noticed the sharp edge in his voice—clipped, judgmental, and unmistakably cold. Though framed as support, it felt more like reprimand.

Tonality speaks louder than words. And his tone pierced through any pretense of care.

This no longer felt like a conversation meant to help me grow or clarify a misunderstanding. It felt confrontational. My resolve to remain open wavered as tension crept back in, clawing at the calm I had worked so hard to find.

I realized the conversation was moving in a direction I was no longer willing to entertain.

I took a steadying breath and spoke.

"This conversation feels like a threat," I said, choosing my words carefully. "You don't know me. You've never checked in, asked how I've been navigating the pandemic, or acknowledged the work I've done supporting clients over the last six months. I don't agree with your observation. Perhaps we should revisit this another time."

I paused, letting the moment settle.

"Thank you for the call," I added, my voice firm but composed. "I'll take time to reflect on what you've shared."

Then I ended the call.

It wasn't easy. But it was necessary.

As I hung up, something shifted inside me—clarity, steadiness, resolve. A mix of boldness and quiet determination replaced the swirl of fear and doubt.

Dignity had stepped forward.

And with it came something unexpected—not anger, not defensiveness, but a question. A question dignity often asks when it is fully present.

Dignity Knows Boundaries

In the quiet that followed, the question surfaced clearly:

Is this the kind of leadership I want to follow?

For years, I had been taught to respect authority without question. To assume the best. To minimize my discomfort. *Your superiors know best,* I was told. *You treat them with respect because that's the right thing to do.*

But as I replayed the conversation, a deeper truth emerged—one that had been buried beneath years of unquestioned beliefs. I wished someone had told me earlier that my feelings mattered too. That respect and dignity, while related, are not the same.

Respect can be offered outwardly.

Dignity must be claimed inwardly.

To be fair, I reminded myself that the world was in upheaval. Covid had reshaped everything, and no one was untouched by its strain. We were all navigating uncertainty in our own ways.

And still, one truth remained clear: Dignity is not circumstantial.

You cannot offer dignity to someone else if you do not first know it within yourself.

This moment was no longer just about one conversation or one person. It was an invitation to honor my own worth while holding space for the shared humanity in others. Dignity, after all, is not about excusing harm or avoiding discomfort—it is about standing firmly in who you are while extending grace where it is deserved.

Alan Cohen said it best, "You can only see in someone else what you see in yourself."

The Root of Dignity

The word *dignity* comes from the Latin *dignitatem*, meaning *worthiness*.

That is where dignity lives—not in external validation, but in the recognition of inherent value.

Dignity is a present emotion. It grounds you. Centers your power. Anchors you in truth.

Related emotions:
Respect • Honor • Humility

How dignity feels in the body:
- Upright, grounded posture
- Steady, expansive breath
- Warmth in the heart space
- Quiet strength rising from within

Dignity can be misunderstood. At times, it disguises itself as pride or ego. But true dignity does not need to prove itself. It isn't loud. It doesn't perform or need an applause.

It allows you to speak clearly, say yes or no without explanation, and remain centered even when misunderstood.

When dignity becomes something we understand about ourselves—not just something we feel—it begins to shape how we live.

Dignity as a Way of Being

Over the past five years, I have devoted myself to honoring dignity as both an emotion and a way of being. Through it, I have learned—deeply—that I matter. That I am worthy.

Dignity freed me from the fog of imposter syndrome and the need for external validation. When I respond from dignity, I no longer demand perfection of myself. I allow growth without shame.

Dignity holds paradox with grace: I can be confident and uncertain. Whole and still becoming. Enough and still growing.

After the feedback about how I showed up on Zoom calls, I began monitoring myself—smiling more, adjusting my tone, second-guessing every move. But instead of expanding, I was shrinking. I wasn't growing—I was performing.

Then clarity arrived.

Dignity doesn't perform.

It grounds.

It calls you home.

I returned to my values: God, Family, Dignity, Adventure, Time, and Trust. The misalignment became undeniable. Two weeks later, I gave my notice.

Dignity as Compass and Communication

Dignity is a compass. It guides decisions that bring peace rather than approval.

Emotional literacy helped me name what I needed to feel whole—but dignity gave me the courage to act on it.

Dignity also reshapes how we communicate.

When I resigned, I had not fully shared my internal struggle with my husband. He was blindsided—and understandably hurt. Dignity in relationship means inclusion. It invites others into the journey, especially when decisions affect them.

That moment revealed something important to me: Dignity does not live in isolation. How we experience it in our closest relationships is often shaped by what we were taught about dignity long before we had words for it.

Why We Hold Back Dignity

Growing up, dignity—especially in women—was often misinterpreted. Confidence was judged. Boundaries were labeled as being cold. Self-worth was mistaken for arrogance. I remember hearing women call other women *"bitches,"* and wondering quietly to myself—not with judgment, but with curiosity—*How do I become that confident?*

Fear of being "too much" led many of us to stay small.

But peace that costs your dignity is not peace—it is strain.

Dignity is not earned.

It is remembered.

You were born with it.

Wisdom Moment

When you lead with dignity, you don't abandon yourself—and you don't diminish others.

You create space for truth, for repair, and for deeper connection.

A Pause for Reflection

Relax into this moment.

Breathe in slowly...and let it go.

Dignity lives in the quiet way you value yourself.

Not in what you achieve—but in how you choose to stand.

Dignity—Your Reflective Journey

1. Self-Worth and Identity

Feels like: Confidence, rootedness, calm

Reveals: You are enough without needing to prove it.

- When do I feel most grounded in my worth?
- What moments cause me to question it?
- What helps me return to truth?

2. Boundaries and Respect

Feels like: Safety, clarity, empowerment

Reveals: What you will and will not tolerate

- Where am I honoring my boundaries?
- Where are they slipping?
- What boundary needs loving firmness?

3. Integrity and Alignment

Feels like: Wholeness, trust, truth

Reveals: When actions align with values

- Where am I living in alignment?
- Where do I feel out of sync?
- What would deeper integrity look like now?

4. Courage and Voice

Feels like: Boldness, presence

Reveals: Your capacity to speak truth

- Where have I silenced myself?

- What am I ready to say?

- How can I honor myself and others?

Wisdom to Carry Forward

- Dignity is not earned—it is remembered.
- True dignity is quiet strength.
- Respect may be given outwardly; dignity must begin within.
- Dignity guides boundaries and values-based decisions.
- It allows clarity without guilt.
- Dignity invites humility, not arrogance.

A GROUNDING WORD

"Strength and dignity are her clothing,
and she smiles at the future.
She opens her mouth in wisdom,
and the teaching of kindness is on her tongue."
—Proverbs 31:25–26

Closing Blessing

You are worthy.
Your pain matters.
Your story matters.
Dignity is not something you earn—it is something you return to.
May this journey help you choose values over fear,
truth over performance, and self-worth over approval.

Journey Three

THE WISDOM OF COURAGE

"Courage is being scared to death, but saddling up anyway."
—John Wayne

When Courage Calls

COURAGE IS A SEVEN-LETTER WORD WITH A MILLION-DOLLAR IMPACT. I read that once, and it never left me.

When we think about courage, we often imagine heroes or dramatic acts—people standing in the spotlight, doing something extraordinary. But courage is not reserved for grand gestures. More often, it lives quietly in ordinary moments, when someone chooses integrity over comfort, truth over approval, or movement over fear.

Abraham Lincoln once said, *"It often requires more courage to dare to do right than to fear to do wrong."* That quote has guided me for more than thirty years.

Courage became one of my core virtues—a compass I return to again and again. It keeps me open to possibilities when the road ahead is unclear. It reminds me that even the smallest bold step, taken without certainty, can become a defining moment in our story.

One such moment arrived when I was seventeen—long before I understood just how often courage would ask me to show up.

The Day Courage Chose Me

It was a beautiful June morning in Liberty, New York—one week before high school graduation. I sat on the stoop of a downtown salon where I had just landed a job. The town was waking up: shop owners unlocking doors, coffee brewing in nearby restaurants, cars easing into motion.

I felt proud. Two weeks into a job I loved, already working as a cosmetologist before I even held my diploma.

And yet, something felt off.

The salon owner hadn't arrived. She had an 8:30 client—she was never late.

Then, unexpectedly, the building owner stepped outside.

"She's not coming back," he said calmly. "Here are the keys. I own the equipment. If you want to open up, go ahead. We'll talk later about your options."

I stared at him, stunned.

I sat there holding the keys, one question circling in my mind: *Do I have the courage to do this?* There wasn't much time to reflect— the first client would be arriving soon.

So I made a decision. *What do I have to lose?*

I knew how to cut hair. Maybe that was enough to begin.

So I opened the door.

I served every client that day as if nothing had changed. When the last appointment left and I locked up, I sat in the barber chair, spun myself once, and whispered, *Is this real?*

I called my dad.

He arrived within the hour—quiet, observant, steady. He took in the shop slowly, nodding as he looked around.

Then he asked a question that changed everything.

"What do you want to do?"

I told him the truth. Owning a business wasn't part of my plan. College was.

He offered something better than certainty. He offered courage with stability.

"Run it for a month," he said. "Build it. If you decide it's not for you, sell it. But give yourself the chance to try."

It wasn't all-or-nothing.

It was one brave step at a time.

A few days later, my first real business meeting took place. My dad and I met with Mike, the building owner—a respected pharmacist in town who believed deeply in young people with vision.

He handed me the lease, looked me in the eyes, and said words I will never forget:

"I believe in you."

That moment planted something deep inside me—not just courage, but confidence.

Courage in Motion

The sun was shining, music filled my car, and I couldn't stop smiling. Three weeks earlier, I had been studying for finals. Now I was a business owner. The contrast felt surreal.

When I unlocked the heavy wooden door—*my* door—and stepped inside, ideas were already flowing.

I picked up the phone and called my best friend.

"You won't believe what happened," I said. "I own the salon. Do you want to come work with me?"

She said yes.

Just like that, we were running a salon.

Each day unfolded like a page being written in real time. I loved doing hair, but I loved even more watching the business come alive—appointments, conversations, laughter.

And the smiles.

People left our little shop feeling seen, cared for, and beautiful.

That first month required courage, stamina, and a growing belief that I was worthy of what stood in front of me. Some mornings, still tucked beneath warm blankets, I would smile and think, *I'm really doing this.*

That door became a symbol. Every time I unlocked it, I felt a surge of pride.

My dad and I painted the walls bright and welcoming. We laid new floors. Every corner reflected ambition.

That summer blurred into joy and bold beginnings.

So I decided to wait on college.

For now, this was working.

Courage Fuels Adventure

Then winter came—and business slowed.

The quiet returned, and with it, reflection.

Before owning the salon, I planned to attend college away from my hometown. Was that still possible? Did I still want it?

One afternoon, sipping tea at the kitchen table, I stared into the bottom of my cup, half-jokingly asking the tea leaves for direction. They were silent, of course.

As I sat pondering, my eyes drifted across the room and landed on a stack of old paper maps—the way my generation once found its way in the world.

I unfolded one and spread it across the table.

And suddenly, a new possibility appeared. Florida.

The sun, the ocean, the familiarity—it stirred something in me. I had been there many times, and it already felt like possibility. A future I could feel but not yet explain.

Courage whispered again: *Let's do it.*

But courage doesn't only ask us to dream.

Sometimes, it asks us to speak.

The Conversation That Required Courage

There was one conversation I still needed to have.

My dad.

Once again, I found myself sitting in the salon chair, slowly spinning, taking in the walls we painted and the business we built.

Is this really the best choice?

The answer came back quietly but clearly: *Yes.*

I invited my dad to lunch the next day at Goody's—our favorite spot up the street.

I arrived early. My palms were sweaty. My legs bounced beneath the table. Guilt and fear churned inside me. My dad had helped me build this. What if he felt disappointed? What if I was walking away from a gift?

His voice echoed in my mind: *Work hard for thirty years, then retire.*

That wasn't the life I saw for myself.

When he walked in, I waved him over. We ordered. I looked into his deep brown eyes—the kind that always seemed to see straight through me—and my heart pounded.

And then I said it.

"Dad...I don't want to own the salon for thirty years and then retire. I'm moving to Florida."

Silence stretched between us.

Finally, he leaned in and said, "You'll need a plan."

That plan set me free.

Within a month, the salon had a new owner.

And I was driving toward a new future.

Courage didn't close a door.

It opened a wider horizon.

The Root of Courage

The word *courage* comes from the Latin *cor*, meaning *heart*.

That is where courage lives—not in the absence of fear, but in the willingness to act with your whole heart even when fear is present.

Courage is a future-focused emotion. It fuels vision, awakens boldness, and invites us to imagine what could be—then take steps toward it, uncertain and unpolished, but purposeful.

Related emotions:
Boldness • Confidence • Trust

How courage feels in the body:
- Energized movement through the body
- Quickened breath high in the chest
- Shoulders squared, posture lifted
- Focused fire in the eyes—even if hands tremble

Courage is often misunderstood. Impulsiveness and stubbornness are sometimes mistaken for bravery.

True courage isn't reckless.

It isn't loud.

It is committed.

Courage lives in the heart because wisdom requires movement.

Courage Isn't a Straight Line

Courage has never followed a straight path in my life.

It has shown up in curves, crossroads, and quiet moments—asking me to rise, reset, and begin again. It has taught me to fail forward and to learn through experience, rather than wait for certainty.

Courage walked beside me through marriage, motherhood, and entrepreneurship.

As a young mother advocating for my son with cerebral palsy, courage became my steady voice in medical meetings. It stood with me in delivery rooms—through surgeries, sleepless nights, and moments that required more strength than I thought I had.

Courage appeared when I dated again after divorce.

When I walked down the aisle again after heartbreak.

When I built businesses—and when I let them go.

To begin again.

To love again after loss.

It asked me to speak on stages.

To share vulnerably.

To move to new towns.

Courage has also taught me how to say goodbye.

It walked beside me as I wrote these pages. Putting this story into words required honesty, vulnerability, and the willingness to be seen without knowing how it would be received. There were moments I hesitated—moments I wondered if my voice mattered, moments I considered staying silent.

But courage reminded me that truth doesn't need permission. It only needs presence.

As I revised this journey, someone dear to me—my beloved friend, the wind beneath my wings—entered hospice care. Before she chose to stop treatment, I believed she would heal. I held hope fiercely.

Now I am learning what it means to release hope with grace.

Courage says: *Be present. Hold her hand. Say what matters. Let your tears fall.*

Watching someone you cherish prepare to leave this world requires a kind of courage that breaks you open—and builds you at the same time.

Letting go of people, roles, or identities that no longer align takes strength.

This is how we create space—for healing, for truth, and for what comes next.

Why We Hold Back from Courage

We all admire courage.

Living it is another matter.

Fear feels safer than failure. So we hesitate. We stall. We ask ourselves:

What if I fail?

What will they think?

What if I'm not enough?

So we stay still.

But courage does not ask us to be fearless.

It invites us to act *with* the fear.

Often, courage looks like small acts:

- Sending the email
- Making the call
- Setting the boundary
- Saying no
- Starting again

If you're hesitating, ask yourself this:

What if the greater risk is not trying at all?

Courage may not promise ease—but it promises growth.

Courage and Thriving

Courage opens the door to exceptional possibility—a life that truly thrives.

Living a thriving life takes courage, because when you are fully alive, you feel more. You question more. You risk more.

Thriving is not numb or safe.

It is awake.

Wisdom Moment

Courage is not the absence of fear—it's choosing to move with it.

Each time you do, you expand who you are becoming.

A Pause for Reflection

Before moving forward, pause for a moment.

Notice where courage is stirring in your own life.

Courage—Your Reflective Journey

1. Fear and Forward Motion

Feels like: Rigidity, dread, worry

Reveals: Your power to act without certainty

- When was the last time I moved forward while afraid?

- What is my fear trying to protect me from?

- What is one small act of courage I can practice today?

2. Risk and Vulnerability

Feels like: Exposure, openness, uncertainty

Reveals: The strength it takes to be seen

- Where am I being called to show up more vulnerably?
- What feels at risk when I'm honest?
- What has vulnerability taught me about courage?

3. Resilience and Grit

Feels like: Inner fire, persistence

Reveals: Courage as a steady refusal to give up

- What challenge have I already survived?
- Where am I stronger than I realize?
- What keeps me moving forward when it's hard?

4. Beginnings and Endings

Feels like: Grief, excitement, release

Reveals: Courage lives in both starting and letting go

- What new chapter am I ready to begin?
- What must I release to move forward?
- How can I honor both the leaving and the arriving?

Wisdom to Carry Forward

- Courage is not the absence of fear—it is movement in its presence.
- Every bold choice begins with the belief that something more is possible.
- Sometimes courage chooses us before we feel ready.
- Letting go is as courageous as beginning.
- You don't need the full map—only the next true step.
- Your story of courage may become the light someone else needs.

A GROUNDING WORD

"So be strong and courageous,
all you who put your hope in the Lord."
—Psalm 31:24

Closing Blessing

May you trust the quiet courage already living within you—
the kind that steadies your feet when the ground shifts.
May you honor the brave choices you've already made,
the doors you opened without certainty,
the goodbyes you said with love,
and the beginnings you dared to imagine.
When fear rises, may courage meet it with compassion.
When grief arrives, may courage soften into presence.
When the path ahead feels unclear, may courage remind you
that you don't need the whole map—only the next true step.
Courage is not something you wait for.
It is something you return to.
It is something you become.

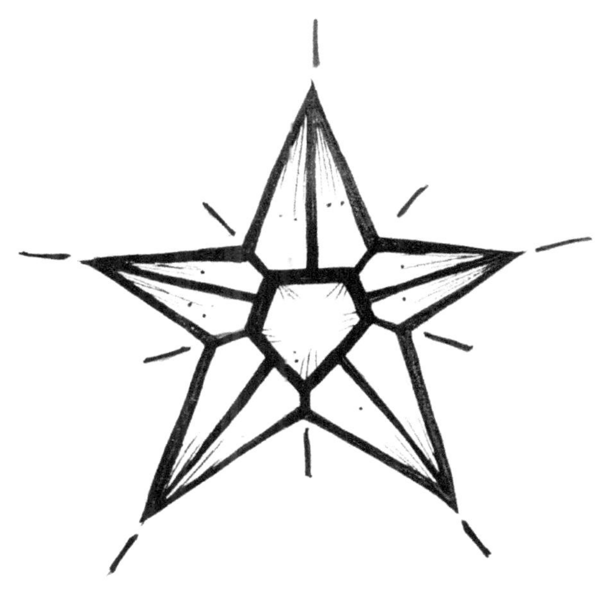

Journey Four

THE WISDOM OF BOLDNESS

*"When I dare to be powerful,
to use my strength in the service of my vision,
then it becomes less and less important whether I am afraid."*
—Audre Lorde

When Boldness Steps Forward

EVERY RING OF WISDOM HAS A QUALITY THAT INVITES US TO BE SEEN.

In this journey, that quality is boldness.

Boldness is not about volume or bravado. It is not about demanding attention or proving worth. Boldness is quieter than that. It is the willingness to step forward without certainty—to say yes before you know how the story will unfold.

Boldness allows opportunity. It asks a simple, courageous question: *Why not me?*

My first meaningful encounter with boldness arrived when I was sixteen.

The Moment Boldness Invited Me In

It was a rainy afternoon when I went to check the mail—almost not bothering, until something nudged me.

Inside the mailbox was a large envelope addressed to me. My heart fluttered as I opened it. It was an invitation to participate in the Miss United Teenager pageant.

My name—on something official.

An 8×10 photo slipped out, one taken at my junior prom. I stared at it, stunned. I looked beautiful. And for the first time, I allowed myself to see it.

Years of self-doubt softened into a single, quiet question:

Why not me?

That envelope sat on my dresser for days. I stared at it, feeling both wonder and uncertainty. With a deep breath, I filled out the form and mailed it back.

That small act—simple on the outside—shifted something deep within me.

Earlier that year, boldness had already asked something of me. My boyfriend didn't want to attend junior prom, so I went alone. In my small town, everyone had a date. Going solo felt like breaking an unspoken rule.

But choosing myself that night opened a door I didn't recognize at the time.

Had I not dared to attend prom alone, I would never have stepped into the possibility of the pageant.

Boldness was choosing to see myself.

Boldness was choosing to say yes.

Freedom Found in Boldness

Submitting the pageant application was bold—and practical. Scholarships were available, and my family couldn't afford the college I dreamed of.

The process stretched me in ways I never expected. I had to secure sponsors, write and deliver a speech, learn choreography, sing in front of an audience, and pose confidently for endless photographs.

Out of eighty contestants, I was the only one with no pageant experience.

That realization hit hard.

The other girls seemed polished, confident—like they belonged on that stage. I felt exposed, uncertain, and now terrified. But I reminded myself: *I earned my place here too.*

So I kept going.

I met girls from across the country and learned something new every day. My roommate from Hamburg, New York, became an anchor—steady, kind, and reassuring. She reminded me that I belonged.

I didn't win the pageant.

But I gained something far more meaningful:

- The freedom to break social norms
- The courage to show up imperfectly
- The confidence to keep going

I didn't come home with a crown.

I came home proud.

Boldness as Attitude

That season taught me something lasting: Boldness doesn't always bring applause—but it always brings growth.

Boldness expands our step forward—moving us beyond "What if?" into "Why not?"

Boldness is not about being fearless. It is about daring to be seen.

Boldness has shown up to support me many times over the years. To push me to trust the unknown and believe that anything is possible. Boldness showed up again—this time through writing.

For more than a decade, I heard the quiet nudge: *Write a book.* Five years ago, I finally listened.

Writing became both mirror and teacher. Each word drew me closer to clarity—revealing where I once held myself back and reintroducing me to a deeply alive, gently caring spirit within.

Even before this manuscript is finished, the act of writing has already changed me.

Boldness is not a single act.

It is a posture.

A way of being.

The Root of Boldness

Boldness comes from the Old English word *beald*, meaning *brave, confident, and strong.*

That is where boldness lives. Like courage, it does not exist in the absence of fear. It exists alongside uncertainty—asking you to move anyway.

Boldness is a future-facing emotion. It fuels vision, awakens possibility, and invites you to discover your unique genius and magic.

Related emotions:

Enthusiasm • Confidence • Zeal

How boldness feels in the body:

- Energized tension in the stomach
- Quickened breath followed by grounding sighs
- A lightness, like readiness to leap
- A quiet inner yes that whispers, *Why not me?*

Boldness is often misunderstood. It can be mistaken for arrogance or righteousness. But true boldness is neither reckless nor careless.

True boldness is willing.
It is intentional.
It is grounded.
Boldness is not impulsive—it is committed.

When Boldness Is Overlooked

Many of us don't think of ourselves as bold.
Yet boldness shows up in ordinary lives every day.
If you have given birth—you are bold.
If you have supported someone through loss—you are bold.
If you honored your truth when it cost you comfort—you are bold.
If you shared who you are with the world—you are bold.
Boldness does not always roar.
Often, it whispers:
This matters. Step forward.

Why We Hold Back from Boldness

So why don't we act boldly more often?
Because fear still whispers:
- What if I fail?
- What if I succeed?
- What will they think?
- What if I'm wrong?

Many of us were taught to be seen and not heard—to stay quiet, agreeable, and small.

Marianne Williamson reminds us, *"Our deepest fear is not that we are inadequate. Our deepest fear is that we are powerful beyond measure.... Your playing small doesn't serve the world."*

Boldness does not require certainty.

It asks only for willingness.

The reward is not always the outcome.

Sometimes, it is the transformation along the way.

Every bold act is a reclaiming—of voice, vision, and value.

Boldness and Thriving

Boldness opens the door to exceptional possibility—a life that truly is becoming.

Living your best life takes courage, but it is sustained by boldness. When you are fully alive, you feel more. You question more. You risk more.

Thriving is not numb or safe.

It is awake.

Wisdom Moment

Boldness is the courage to be seen as you are, not as you've been conditioned to be.

When you choose boldness, you give yourself permission to live fully expressed.

A Pause for Reflection

Before turning inward, pause for a moment.

Notice where boldness may be inviting you forward.

Boldness—Your Reflective Journey

1. Invitation and Self-Doubt

Feels like: Curiosity, disbelief, resistance

Reveals: Recognition of worth and potential

- What opportunity both excites and scares me?
- Where have I dismissed myself too quickly?
- What changes if I believe I am enough?

2. Standing Out in Small Moments

Feels like: Embarrassment, defiance, inner rebellion

Reveals: Boldness begins by breaking quiet rules

- When have I chosen my own path?
- What does honoring myself require right now?
- What small act changed everything?

3. Facing the Unknown

Feels like: Faith, uncertainty, hesitation

Reveals: Boldness shows up—not off

- What stretched me beyond comfort?
- What helped me keep going?
- How did I grow?

4. Belonging Without Permission

Feels like: Insecurity, comparison, judgment

Reveals: Belonging begins within

- Where am I waiting to be chosen?
- What part of me deserves celebration?
- What shifts when I claim my worth?

Wisdom to Carry Forward

- Boldness is not bravado—it is quiet conviction.
- Small yeses can lead to profound change.
- Experience is not required—presence is.
- Not winning does not mean losing.
- Boldness grows through risk and truth.
- You do not need permission to be bold.
- Even when fear whispers, boldness answers, *You belong here.*

A GROUNDING WORD

"The righteous are as bold as a lion."
—Proverbs 28:1

Closing Blessing

May you trust the boldness already alive in you—
the quiet strength that doesn't need approval to begin.
May you honor the small yeses that changed your life,
and the brave moments when you chose yourself
even when it felt uncomfortable, unfamiliar, or unseen.
When doubt returns, may you meet it with dignity.
When comparison rises, may you return to your worth.
When fear whispers, may boldness answer:
This matters. Step forward.

Journey Five

<hr>

THE WISDOM OF FORGIVENESS

"When we realize that we are all sinners needing forgiveness,
it will be easy for us to forgive others."
—Mother Teresa

When Forgiveness Begins

Every Ring of Wisdom holds a place where we begin to become aware of what hurt has to tell us.

In this journey, that place is forgiveness.

Forgiveness is not a light switch you flip.

It is a slow walk.

A gradual untangling of expectation from reality—of separating who we hoped people would be from who they actually were. Very human. Very flawed. Just like us.

Forgiveness rarely arrives all at once.

Some days the hurt rests quietly. Other days it lives deep in the body—tightness in the chest, a clenched jaw, shallow breath, a surge of anger or quiet agony. Our cells hold memory. Healing asks us to listen rather than rush, to notice rather than numb.

When forgiveness is avoided, something else takes its place. Denial often shows up as irritability, resentment, bitterness, emotional exhaustion, and a heaviness that settles into the soul. We may appear fine on the outside while feeling guarded, restless, and spiritually distant within.

Unforgiveness hardens the heart not because we are weak but because we are protecting pain we do not yet feel safe enough to face.

Before forgiveness is possible, we must be willing to name what was unjust. That requires allowing the emotions circling the wound—anger, grief, disappointment, sadness—to rise without judgment.

God does not ask us to bypass our pain.

He invites us to bring it into the light.

I know this from experience.

Becoming the "Proud Owner" of Anger

By my teenage years, I often described myself as the proud owner of a car called *anger*.

It was painted in resentment, dented with sadness, and fueled by blame and bitterness. I did not know another way to be.

I had inherited my mother's rage and my father's distance. I felt abandoned and responsible all at once. I wanted someone to protect me—and when no one did, I decided I would protect myself.

So I built armor from sarcasm, overachieving, and anger.

Forgiveness was never modeled. I never heard the word *sorry*. My father's mantra echoed loudly: *I don't get mad—I get even.*

On the outside, I functioned. I was very careful that no one saw my anger. I was also afraid of it. I saw anger destroy people, and I wasn't going to let that happen in my life. So I became a people pleaser, indifferent to what mattered to me. Creating a protective shell of "I don't care what anyone thinks." On the inside, I was a tangle of unprocessed hurt.

It was not until after two painful divorces in my early twenties that I finally sat across from a counselor and began to understand how deeply the previous decade had carved into my heart.

Therapy became sacred ground—a place where truth could surface and healing could begin.

I started naming what had been true:

- My parents had been reckless and selfish in ways that deeply impacted us.
- My sister's father disappeared from her life entirely.
- The little girl in me never had a safe place to feel what she felt.
- I lived in this existence, unsafe, scared, and hypervigilant.

At first, acknowledging these truths felt like betrayal. Like disloyalty. Like being ungrateful or "too negative."

Then my counselor offered a reframe that changed everything:

I was not betraying anyone.

I was finally acknowledging my pain.

Anger was not my problem.

It was my protector.

Forgiveness Is Not Avoidance

I had been taught that anger was dangerous and wrong. So I tried to skip straight to forgiveness.

That was not forgiveness.

That was avoidance dressed up as virtue.

Real forgiveness does not bypass pain.

It walks through it.

I often describe that season as peeling back an onion.

For years, I wrapped myself in layers of protection:

- *They did the best they could* (true—and not the whole story).
- *It wasn't that bad.*
- *Other people had it worse.*
- *If I'm angry, I'm a bad daughter.*
- *Time heals all wounds.*

Those layers once kept me safe.

Eventually, they began to rot me from the inside.

Layer by layer, I peeled back the truth. And beneath it was raw, unfiltered hurt.

Here is what I had to learn:

Until you have the courage to feel anger about what hurt you, you cannot experience freedom.

Anger is not the opposite of forgiveness.

It is often the doorway to it.

The Practice That Softened My Heart

One gentle practice that supported my healing was Hoʻoponopono:

I'm sorry.

Please forgive me.

Thank you.

I love you.

Hoʻoponopono is a traditional Hawaiian practice of reconciliation, rooted in the belief that healing occurs through repentance, forgiveness, gratitude, and love.

What moved me most was its gentleness.

You do not need to feel ready.

You do not need to believe it fully.

You simply practice.

I once believed that forgiving meant giving others power while I continued to hurt. Over time, I learned the truth:

Forgiveness is not something you do for others.

It is something you do for yourself.

Practiced consistently, this ritual loosened my grip. Emotional energy began to move. My nervous system softened.

Forgiveness did not happen instantly.

But it happened honestly.

The Root of Forgiveness

The Old English word *forgiefan* means:
- To give or grant
- To remit a debt
- To give up completely

Forgiveness lives in the present moment. It is the decision to stop carrying something that is breaking your body, your heart, and your spirit.

Forgiveness is not pretending it didn't happen.

Forgiveness is not saying it was okay.

Forgiveness is not granting permission for harm to continue.

Forgiveness sounds more like this:

You no longer have power over me. I am free.

In the body, forgiveness feels like softening.

The breath lengthens.

The chest opens.

The heart releases its armor.

Forgiveness does not erase the past.

It loosens its grip.

The Cost of Holding On

Most of us were never taught how forgiveness supports health. We were simply taught to say *sorry*.

But real sorrow is not a word.

It is awareness, accountability, and change.

For me, chronic anger kept my nervous system locked in fight-or-flight. Over time, this contributed to depression, exhaustion, and disconnection from who I really was.

As I practiced forgiveness—journaling, breathing, reflecting—my body began to calm. Stress softened. Joy and connection slowly returned.

Your body hears every thought you think.

Forgiveness is not only a spiritual act.

It is profound self-care.

Wisdom Moment

Forgiveness does not change what happened.

It changes what you carry forward.

It creates space—for peace, for love, for freedom to rise.

A Pause for Reflection

Before turning inward, pause for a moment.

Notice what your body is holding—and what

it may be ready to release.

Forgiveness—Your Reflective Journey

1. Naming the Wound

Feels like: Anger, grief, sadness

Reveals: What needs acknowledgment

- What still hurts when I think about this?

- What truth have I avoided naming?

- What emotion needs space right now?

2. Anger as Protector

Feels like: Tension, vigilance, intensity

Reveals: How I learned to survive

- How has anger protected me?

- When did it become too heavy to carry alone?

- What would safety feel like now?

3. Self-Forgiveness

Feels like: Humility, relief, tenderness

Reveals: Grace begins within

- Where do I need to forgive myself?

- What unrealistic standard am I releasing?

- What does compassion toward myself look like?

4. Choosing Freedom

Feels like: Softening, breath, release

Reveals: Forgiveness as liberation

- What would letting go—even a little—offer me?

- What does freedom feel like in my body?

- What am I ready to stop carrying?

Wisdom to Carry Forward

- Forgiveness is not a feeling—it is a choice.
- You cannot heal what you refuse to name.
- Anger is often the doorway, not the destination.
- Self-forgiveness is an act of humility, not weakness.
- Forgiveness does not excuse harm—it releases you from it.
- Freedom grows where honesty is allowed.

A GROUNDING WORD

"Be kind and compassionate to one another, forgiving each other, just as in Christ God forgave you."
—Ephesians 4:32

Closing Blessing

May you release what no longer belongs to you.
May you soften toward your own humanity with the same grace
you long to offer others.
May forgiveness arrive in its own time—
without force, without shame.
May your body remember peace.
May your heart feel lighter.
And may freedom meet you gently, exactly where you are.

Journey Six

THE WISDOM OF SELF-CARE

"Self-care is not a waste of time; self-care is an investment."
—Wayne Dyer

When Self-Care Becomes Necessary

EVERY RING OF WISDOM HAS A PLACE WHERE WE ARE ASKED TO SLOW DOWN.

In this journey, that place is self-care.

For much of my life, I believed self-care was optional—something reserved for people with fewer responsibilities and more margin than I had. If you had told me decades ago that I needed more self-compassion, I likely would have laughed and said, "Sure—let me just lease out my children and pencil in a spa day."

Back then, self-care felt indulgent. Frivolous. Almost irresponsible.

The truth was, I believed putting myself first was selfish. My life revolved around being everything for everyone else—the present parent, the committed partner, the reliable business owner, the dependable friend. I wore exhaustion like a badge of honor, proof that I was doing enough.

But constantly giving without replenishing doesn't always end in collapse.

Sometimes it ends quietly.

One day, you realize the vibrant, joyful version of yourself has been replaced by someone existing on fumes.

I didn't fall apart—I simply began to wonder where I had gone.

Oh Self-Care, Where Art Thou?

My awakening wasn't dramatic. It came as a slow, undeniable realization that the way I was living was unsustainable.

I began with small shifts:

- Moments of stillness instead of constant multitasking
- Saying no without explanation
- Allowing rest without justification

I learned something essential: Being lazy is not failure. Allowing the emotion to be helpful, not negative, like most feel it is. I heard it so much growing up, "Lazy people get nothing done." Being lazy gives the body and mind time to just be, with no guilt or desire to take action. Recuperating from hard work.

"Periods of wholesome laziness, after days of energetic effort, will wonderfully tone up the mind and body."—Grenville Kleiser

Self-care is rarely polished or glamorous. It is uncomfortable at first. It asks you to listen when your body says stop. It requires boundaries. It invites you to offer yourself the same grace you give everyone else.

Ironically, caring for myself did not diminish my capacity to care for others—it deepened it. When I began tending to my own wellness, my love became steadier, my energy more generous, and my presence more authentic.

What surprised me most was how unfamiliar this felt—because self-care was never modeled for me growing up.

Redefining What Self-Care Really Means

Growing up, self-care was not part of our vocabulary. In the 1970s and '80s, most women I knew were too busy holding everything together to name their needs.

My mother, like many women of her generation, carried strength through appearance. She had style, confidence, and poise. To my young eyes, that looked like self-care.

But over time, I learned that caring for yourself runs far deeper than how you appear.

True self-care is not about how you look.

It is about how you feel.

For a long time, I equated self-care with presentation—hair done, makeup on, showing up composed no matter what was happening inside. Eventually, life asked for more honesty.

What if caring for ourselves isn't selfish but sacred?

The Evolution of Self-Care

Today, self-care has reclaimed its rightful place.

Not indulgent.

Not earned.

Essential.

Self-care is tending to your physical, emotional, mental, and spiritual well-being with intention. It is recognizing that you are human—not a machine designed to produce without rest.

Self-care evolves as we do. Each season of life asks for different rhythms, different boundaries, different forms of nourishment.

Wisdom is knowing when to adjust.

Listening to the Body's Wisdom

One of the most profound lessons self-care taught me came through my body.

In my early forties, anxiety and emotional volatility intensified. I assumed something was wrong with me. I didn't yet understand the impact of hormonal imbalance.

Out of desperation, I fell to my knees and prayed: *"God, I need help. I don't want to live like this."*

That prayer led me—unexpectedly—to answers.

Hormone testing revealed severe imbalance. With proper support, nutrition, and treatment, my clarity returned. My energy stabilized. My spirit softened.

That experience taught me this:

The body is not betraying us.

It is communicating.

Self-care means listening.

Self-Care and Sustainability

Self-care is not about doing less out of avoidance.

It is about doing life from a place of sustainability, reverence, and truth.

When we ignore our needs, the body keeps score. When we listen, it responds with resilience.

Self-care is how wisdom stays alive in the Ring.

Wisdom Moment

Self-care is not selfish.

It is the foundation that sustains everything you give.

A Pause for Reflection

Let what you've read settle—not only in your mind,

but in your body.

These reflections are not a test.

They are an invitation to notice what is true,

and to meet it with curiosity, honesty, and care.

Self-Care—Your Reflective Journey

1. Overgiving and Reconnection

Feels like: Exhaustion, depletion

Reveals: Where you've abandoned yourself in service of others

- Where am I overextending without replenishing?
- What part of me is asking to be restored?
- What would gentle reconnection look like this week?

2. Guilt and Permission

Feels like: Guilt, resistance

Reveals: Inherited beliefs about worth and having a lazy day.

- What messages did I receive about rest?
- How does guilt show up when I slow down?
- What would permission feel like in my body?

3. Stillness and Listening

Feels like: Quiet, tenderness

Reveals: Inner wisdom

- When do I feel most at peace?
- What arises when I allow stillness?
- What have I been too busy to hear?

4. Boundaries and Self-Respect

Feels like: Strength, discomfort

Reveals: How you honor your energy

- Where do I need a clearer boundary?
- What does saying no protect?
- How does my body respond when I honor myself?

Wisdom to Carry Forward

- Self-care is essential, not indulgent.
- Being lazy can also be productive.
- Boundaries are acts of dignity.
- Small, consistent care creates lasting change.
- Your body carries wisdom. Listen.
- Caring for yourself deepens your capacity to care for others.

A GROUNDING WORD

*"Come to me, all who labor and are heavy laden,
and I will give you rest."*
—Matthew 11:28

Closing Blessing

Self-care is not a luxury—it is a foundation.
It is how you honor the body, mind,
and spirit you have been entrusted with.
When you choose rest, you are not stepping away from life.
You are returning to it—with clarity, presence, and strength.
May you allow rest without guilt.
May you listen to what your body and soul are asking for.
May you release the belief that exhaustion is proof of worth.
Carry this wisdom forward as a reminder:
Caring for yourself is not stepping back
—it is preparing to live fully.

78

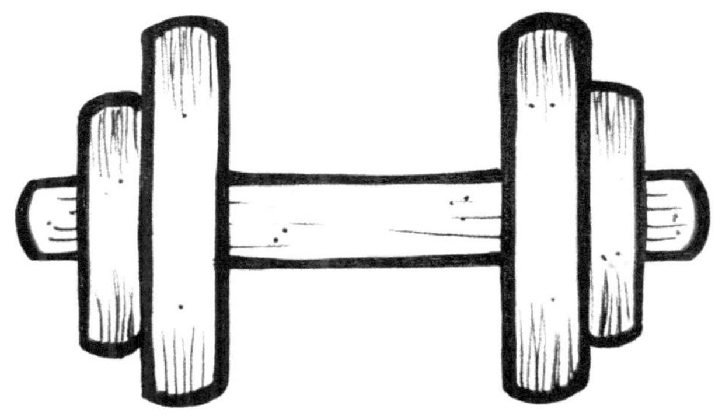

Journey Seven

THE WISDOM OF
PHYSICAL HEALTH

"Your body has natural healing capacities that nobody in the field of medicine can pretend to understand."
—Wayne Dyer

When the Body Speaks

Every Ring of Wisdom has a place where truth becomes tangible—where wisdom is not only understood, but lived.

Physical health lives in the body, where every other wisdom is carried. Emotions settle here. Dignity is felt here. Courage moves from here. Boldness is embodied here. Forgiveness either softens or tightens this space. Self-care sustains it.

For much of my life, I treated physical health as something to manage—something I could outwork, outthink, or push through. I didn't understand yet that the body is not something we control or manage. It is something we partner with.

This journey explores what happens when we stop treating the body as something to manage or push through and begin honoring it as a messenger—one that holds memory, wisdom, and deep intelligence.

This journey is an invitation to listen.

My Health Journey

When I started writing this book five years ago, I felt strong—physically, mentally, and emotionally. I've never been a gym rat, and I've never chased perfection. But I have always been intentional about one thing: eating well. I'll admit it—I'm a little obsessive about it, in the best possible way.

Healthy eating was a core value in my upbringing. My grandparents lived an "off-the-land" lifestyle—big gardens, cows, chickens, rabbits, pigs. Our food was fresh, natural, and simple. Their reverence for nourishment left an imprint on me that never faded.

I carried that value into my own family.

It wasn't always easy. I loved preparing food from our small garden—nothing like my grandparents had, but deeply meaningful to me. It was time-consuming, yet the satisfaction of growing something with my own hands and feeding my family from it was pure euphoria. Organic and natural foods can be expensive, and preparing real meals takes time. Still, it was a commitment I was willing to make. Sundays became our rhythm—my kids and I meal-prepping for the week. We chopped vegetables, baked healthier snacks, portioned dinners, and made weekday choices easier.

Looking back, it was worth every bit of effort. My kids—now grown—are mindful of what they put into their bodies. They'll tell you honestly: It takes time, and it costs more. But they also know what it feels like to be nourished.

And as I write this chapter, my mom is eighty-one years old, on no medication, and still a full-time caregiver. She remains one of my steady inspirations for staying active and awake to life.

Life in Motion

Movement was simply part of my childhood. Living in the country meant biking or walking wherever we needed to go. It wasn't exercise—it was life.

I played softball, soccer, and basketball. I was outside whenever I could be—snowmobiling, riding motorcycles, chasing fresh air and adventure.

As I grew older, I held on to that same mindset: Stay active in ways that feel like joy.

Today, that looks like swimming, tennis, walking, biking, hiking, kayaking—and watching the pickleball craze with curiosity. Yoga has become a favorite—not only for strength and flexibility, but for what it does to my breath. It brings me back to center.

For me, staying active has never been about fitness alone.

It's freedom.

It's joy.

It's connection.

I believed this rhythm would always be there—until my body taught me otherwise. Health has a way of becoming visible when it is disrupted, when the familiar suddenly disappears.

The Day the World Lost Its Flavor

When I contracted Covid-19, I never imagined it would take two senses I had always taken for granted: smell and taste.

At first, I minimized it. Compared to what others were facing, this felt small.

But as days turned into weeks, the loss hit deeper than I expected.

Taste disappeared first. Eating became mechanical—food was fuel without pleasure. I missed the layering of flavor, the depth of roasted garlic, the way spices unfold.

Losing my sense of smell gutted me.

Smell was grounding. It was safety. It was home.

Without it, my world felt unfamiliar. I couldn't smell coffee brewing, fresh-cut grass, or rain-soaked earth. Twice, I reheated coffee on the stove without realizing it was burning—until my husband rushed in shouting.

That fear settled in my chest like a stone.

I grieved the loss of smell the way you grieve a friend. Quietly. Deeply.

How It Shifted My Body and Mood

Over time, losing smell and taste affected more than food—it affected my mood.

Without sensory comfort, I reached for what I could still feel: sugar, starch, eventually whiskey. The results were real—weight gain, less muscle tone, more alcohol, and more depression than I anticipated.

Then came a bright spot: my puppy.

She brought joy and movement back into my days. Daily walks kept me afloat. Even when I couldn't smell nature, my memory remembered what it used to feel like—and that memory carried me.

Healthy living, I learned, is not static.

It evolves with life.

The Root of Physical Health

Physical health is not perfection.

It is relationship.

It is the ongoing conversation between body, mind, emotion, and spirit—and our willingness to listen.

Related emotions:

Vitality • Safety • Groundedness • Trust

How physical health feels in the body:

- Steady energy rather than spikes
- Ease in breath and movement

• A sense of partnership instead of pressure
• Faster recovery after stress
The body does not betray us.
It communicates.

When Physical Health Is Misunderstood

Physical health is often misunderstood as something to conquer—or something to avoid thinking about altogether.

I resisted mammograms for years. I felt healthy and didn't like the process.

My husband delayed seeing an orthopedic doctor, believing he could push through pain—until he needed double hip replacement.

Avoidance feels easier than knowing.

I have also witnessed the cost of ignoring the body through a family member who numbed fear with alcohol and cigarettes instead of seeking care. At sixty-nine, she had a stroke, was diagnosed with late-stage lung cancer, and passed two weeks later.

I share this gently, but truthfully:
Your health affects more than you.

Wisdom Moment

Your body is always speaking—through energy, tension, and ease.

The wisdom of physical health is learning to listen, honor, and respond with care.

A Pause for Reflection

Physical health asks us to pause—not to judge

what we've done wrong, but to notice what

our body has been asking for all along.

The wisdom is not in doing more.

It is in listening sooner.

Physical Health—Your Reflective Journey

1. Nourishment and Care

Feels like: Intention, responsibility

Reveals: How daily choices shape long-term well-being

- How do I currently nourish my body?

- What habits support my energy—and which quietly

  drain it?

- What small shift would feel supportive right now?

2. Movement and Vitality

Feels like: Freedom, connection

Reveals: That movement sustains life rather than punishes the body

- When do I feel most alive in my body?
- What kind of movement feels joyful rather than forced?
- How has my relationship with movement changed over time?

3. Listening to the Body

Feels like: Awareness, sensitivity

Reveals: That the body speaks long before it breaks down

- What signals has my body been sending?
- Where have I ignored discomfort or fatigue?
- What would it look like to respond with care instead of pressure?

4. Health and Wholeness

Feels like: Integration, compassion

Reveals: That physical, emotional, and spiritual health are inseparable

- How do stress or emotions show up in my body?
- What support do I need right now?
- What would honoring my body look like in this season?

Wisdom to Carry Forward

- Your body is not something to manage—it's something to partner with.
- Small, consistent choices create lasting vitality.
- Movement, nourishment, and rest are forms of self-respect.
- Ignoring your body whispers often leads to louder signals.
- Caring for your health today is an investment in how you live tomorrow.

A GROUNDING WORD

"Beloved, I pray that all may go well with you and that you may be in good health, just as it is well with your soul."
—3 John 1:2

Closing Blessing

You matter. Your body matters. Your physical health matters.
May you treat your body as a companion.
May you honor its signals with dignity and care.
And as you carry this wisdom forward, may you remember:
The Ring of Wisdom is not only something we understand
—it is something we live, breath by breath, day by day,
within our own bodies.

Journey Eight

THE WISDOM OF MENTAL HEALTH

"Not until we are lost do we begin to understand ourselves."
—Henry David Thoreau

When the Mind Enters the Ring

Every Ring of Wisdom holds a place where clarity feels just out of reach.

In this journey, that place is mental health.

Mental health is not only about what we think—it is about how we experience life from the inside. It shapes how we interpret the world, how we relate to ourselves, and how we carry our stories forward.

For many of us, mental health is invisible until it isn't. It becomes noticeable when the noise grows louder, when the fog thickens, or when the effort to appear "fine" takes more energy than we have left.

This journey is about naming what lives beneath the surface—and learning how to come home to yourself when the mind feels like unfamiliar territory.

A Roller Coaster Through the Fog

For years, my mind felt like a place I didn't recognize.

Each jarring turn left me longing for the ride to stop, but my pleas seemed to go unheard. The rattling of the tracks mirrored the chaos inside me—negative voices growing louder with every plunge.

My body became a battlefield. Waves of nausea churned in my stomach. Fear disoriented me. My chest tightened. My breath shortened. I was desperate for clarity or control.

This was not the thrilling rush people sign up for. It was relentless. And even when the ride "stopped," the emotions didn't.

Sadness.

Anger.

Anxiety.

Despair.

They clung to me like fog that refused to lift.

My mental health didn't just live in my mind—it lived in my body. Sleep became elusive. Appetite unreliable. Tasks that once felt routine began to feel monumental.

For over thirty-four years, I cycled through seasons of what I believed were anxiety and depression. I asked myself endlessly:

What is wrong with me?

Why can't I escape this?

I didn't yet know that I was trapped in emotional saturation—and had never been taught how to step off the ride.

If you've ever felt this way, what came next may feel familiar.

My Silent Battle

For much of my life, I lived a double existence.

Outwardly, I smiled, met expectations, and achieved professional success. I looked "fine."

Inside, I was screaming for help.

I wanted to say, *I'm not okay. I need someone to listen.*

But fear kept me silent.

I feared judgment.

I feared being seen as unreliable.

I feared being avoided altogether.

As a child and teenager, I endured an experience no one should have to carry—one that shattered my understanding of safety and trust. It disrupted my relationship with my body, with men, and with the world's ability to protect me.

I buried it.

So deeply that sadness became familiar—quiet, heavy, normalized.

Imposter syndrome took root. I overperformed. I blurred boundaries. I stayed busy. I curated how others saw me while suppressing who I truly was.

And deep down, I didn't believe my own press.

Breaking the Silence

Looking back, I see how costly my silence was.

Mental health struggles are not abstract ideas—they are embodied experiences. You do not need a diagnosis to know when something inside you is asking for care.

If you recognize yourself here, please hear this:

You are not weak for needing help.

Speaking to someone—a trusted friend, a pastor, a counselor, a therapist, a doctor—can be the first step toward reclaiming yourself. It is not an instant fix.

But it is movement.

One honest step at a time.

The Root of Mental Health

Mental health is our overall emotional, psychological, and relational well-being. Everyone has mental health, and it shifts across seasons of life.

Mental illness, while related, involves diagnosable conditions that significantly interfere with daily functioning and often require professional treatment.

This distinction matters.

Many people suffer quietly, believing they must push through, when what they truly need is support.

Mental health is also deeply connected to the body. Hormones, nutrients, sleep, trauma, and nervous-system regulation all play a role. Healing is whole-person work.

But our culture has told a different story.

When Mental Health Is Misunderstood

Our struggle with mental health is often misunderstood as something we should "think our way out of."

So we analyze.

We replay conversations.

We search for answers in noise.

But healing often begins when we return to the body.

Stepping out of your head is not avoidance.

It is presence.

The tight chest.

The lump in the throat.

The flutter in the stomach.

These sensations are not enemies.

They are messages asking to be felt.

Listening to them is how we find our way back home.

A Bridge Back to Self

One of the simplest practices that changed everything for me was learning to pause.

The 90-Second Pause

When you feel yourself spiraling:

Pause.

Bring your awareness from thought into sensation.

Ask: *What am I feeling—and where do I feel it?*

Name it.

Breathe into it.

Allow it—without fixing.

That pause is not small.

It is the doorway back to yourself. And from that place, healing begins to unfold—quietly, steadily, honestly.

The Freedom Journey

Over the past few years, my mental health has softened into strength—less driven by fear, more guided by awareness.

I still have off days—but I no longer fight them. Instead of judging, I name what's true. I tend to my nervous system. I make space. That single shift—naming instead of judging—changed my life.

I learned to disentangle emotions from identity.

They are messengers.

Not definitions.

Choice returned.

Dignity returned.

Freedom followed.

Mental health is not about control.

It is about relationship with ourselves.

Wisdom Moment

Mental health is not about fixing yourself—it's about understanding yourself. When you learn to listen instead of judge, healing begins.

A Pause for Reflection

Take a moment.

Let what you've read settle—not in your mind alone,

but in your body and breath.

There is no need to fix anything.

Simply notice what is present.

Mental Health—Your Reflective Journey

1. When Emotions Feel Too Big to Hold

Feels like: Overwhelm, flooding, pressure

Reveals: Something needs acknowledgment, not fixing

- What am I feeling right now?
- Where do I feel it in my body?
- What would giving myself permission to sit with the vastness of big emotions do for me?

2. When You Feel Numb

Feels like: Disconnection, shutdown

Reveals: Emotional saturation or self-protection

- When did I disconnect?

- What feels unsafe to feel?

- What helps me gently reconnect?

3. The Weight of Proving Worth

Feels like: Pressure, never-enough

Reveals: A belief that worth must be earned

- Where did this belief begin?

- What would "enough" feel like?

- How can I offer myself acceptance?

4. The Voice of Shame

Feels like: Shrinking, secrecy

Reveals: Old stories that were never yours

- Whose voice do I hear?
- What truth replaces it?
- What would compassion say?

Wisdom to Carry Forward

- Mental health is embodied—mind and body are inseparable.
- Silence may feel protective, but truth creates freedom.
- Emotional literacy restores dignity and agency.
- Boundaries support mental health.
- Support is strength, not weakness.
- Healing is not linear—but it is possible.

A GROUNDING WORD

*"You will keep in perfect peace those whose minds are steadfast,
because they trust in you."*
—Isaiah 26:3

Closing Blessing

May you learn to listen to your inner world without fear.
May the fog lift gently—in your breath, your body, your thoughts.
May support meet you when you need it.
May dignity guide you home to yourself.
You matter.
Your mind matters.
Your healing matters.

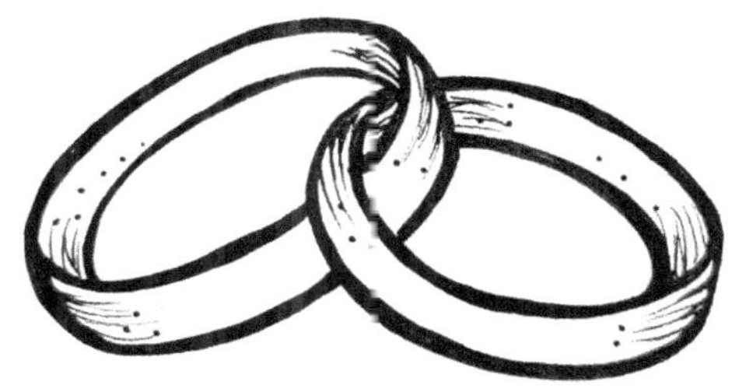

Journey Nine

THE WISDOM OF MARRIAGE

"A great marriage is not when the 'perfect couple' comes together.
It is when an imperfect couple learns to enjoy their differences."
—Dave Meurer

When Marriage Becomes a Teacher

EVERY RING OF WISDOM HAS A PLACE WHERE LOVE IS TESTED—NOT BY ROMANCE, BUT BY REALITY.

In this journey, that place is marriage.

It's safe to say there are tens of thousands of books written about marriage. I know this because I've read many of them—and because I've lived a great deal of it.

After thirty-four years of marriage (and two marriages before that), I can say this with certainty:

Marriage is not one-size-fits-all.

Growing up, I witnessed marriage in many forms. Some were filled with warmth, laughter, and mutual respect. Others were marked by pain, anger, silence, separation, and grief that seemed to linger long after doors closed.

I saw couples who felt like soulmates—shared glances, easy laughter, a deep sense of *we*.

And I saw the other side—where love hardened under unmet expectations, unspoken resentment, or broken trust. Some homes were loud. Some were painfully quiet. In both, the ache was unmistakable.

Those early observations shaped me more than I realized. They taught me that love alone isn't always enough. Marriage requires effort, patience, and a willingness to grow—especially through storms.

They also left me with a question that followed me into adulthood:

If marriage can be so many things—joyful and painful, hopeful and heartbreaking—what will it be for me?

I wondered if there was a handbook. A step-by-step way of growing together. An outline for me to follow and learn from.

Marriage Has No Handbook

What I learned is this: There is no handbook with step-by-step instructions guaranteeing success.

Marriage, like life, is fluid. It evolves because people evolve.

Coming from a broken home, I learned early that divorce is not just legal or financial—it is deeply emotional. Anxiety, anger, grief, loneliness, depression, and identity loss arrive together, often without language to process them.

For years, I fought sadness. I feared that if I stayed with it too long, it would pull me under.

What I didn't yet understand was this:

Sadness is not the enemy.

It shows us what matters.

It deserves to be felt—not avoided.

Sadness will always be a part of life—within marriage and far beyond it. What I have learned over time is that sadness is not a state from which we are meant to make permanent decisions. When we are sad, feeling and logic often compete with one another. The heart is tender. The nervous system is activated. Clarity can feel distant.

Sadness does not ask to be rushed.

It asks to be honored.

It asks to be nourished with compassion, patience, and time.

When sadness is acknowledged rather than suppressed, it becomes informative rather than overwhelming. It slows us down long enough to notice what hurts, what is missing, and what matters most. Only then can wisdom begin to form.

This is where the destiny of a marriage is shaped.

The future of a marriage has much to do with emotional agility—how well we understand, express, and regulate what we feel. When emotions are ignored or bypassed, resentment quietly takes root. And resentment doesn't stay in the mind—it settles into the body and the relationship.

Strong marriages thrive on communication and conversation—not blaming, fixing, or yelling, but listening, naming, and returning to one another with honesty.

Marriage is not static. It is a journey with no map.

What matters most is not perfection but the intention you bring with you.

Going to Chapel

My mother used to sing "Going to the Chapel" when I was little. I took in every word with the innocence of a girl who believed love, once chosen, was forever. At nineteen, I fell in love.

He was energetic, handsome, and seemingly ready to build a life with me. I was young, hopeful, and deeply determined that my marriage would look different from what I had witnessed growing up. I wanted to do it right. I wanted it to last.

A year into our marriage, we welcomed a child—and everything shifted.

I poured myself into becoming the perfect wife and mother. I managed the house, paid the bills, kept everything running, and tried to look composed when he came home. I believed—truly—that if I worked hard enough, I could hold us together.

What I didn't fully understand at the time was that, even as I stood married, a quiet belief lived inside me: *This won't work out.* I fought that thought constantly.

I told myself, *No—my marriage is different. I will never get divorced. No matter what.*

There was a kind of innocence in that resolve. Naivety, even. But it shaped everything that followed.

Because of that story in my mind, I became obsessed with doing everything right. I never said no. When I felt diminished, I didn't push back—I got smaller. I learned to scan the room, the tone, the mood, trying to anticipate what would keep the peace.

When anger showed up, I turned it inward.

What did I do wrong?

Why is he so upset?

How can I fix this?

I tried harder. I quieted myself. And slowly, without having words for it, I disappeared inside the marriage. Loneliness crept in—not because I was alone, but because I no longer felt safe being myself.

I didn't yet have the language to name what was happening. I only knew that I felt scared, confused, and unsure of who I was becoming.

And in trying so desperately to save the marriage, I lost myself.

Over time, love gave way to jealousy, control, and fear. And I learned a painful truth: when a marriage ends without healing, the longing to be loved does not disappear—it only grows louder.

I didn't leave that marriage whole. I left wounded, hopeful, and still searching for safety.

From the Frying Pan into the Fire

After my divorce, longing to be loved again, I rushed into another marriage.

It lasted six months.

We had also gone into business together—buying a bakery—which complicated everything. Sharing a business ownership inside a collapsing marriage is like throwing gasoline on a fire.

That second marriage taught me how desperation can blind us to warning signs we should honor.

Still, even there, lessons lived.

With the support of family and friends, I slowly found my way out of anxiety, fear, guilt, and shame. Sadness grew into resilience. Anger softened through gratitude.

And I began to like myself again.

Hard lessons.

Necessary ones.

Oh Dear Lord, Help Me

After two failed marriages, the thought of a healthy relationship felt terrifying.

I carried shame.

And I had children.

So I prayed honestly:

Dear Lord, I'm clearly not a good judge of character. Please help me. I don't want to be alone forever. When I meet the man I'm meant to spend my life with, let him be kind, patient, and loving—to me and my children.

Months later, a friend invited me out dancing.

The invitation stirred two opposing emotions in my body at the same time—cynicism and hope. Cynicism, because disappointment had become familiar. Hope, because some small part of me still wanted to believe life held more than survival.

I hesitated. I hadn't taken time away from my children for anything like this in a long time. My world had narrowed to routines, responsibilities, and the quiet walls of motherhood. I wasn't sure I even remembered how to be *me* outside of that role—or if that version of me still existed.

I was twenty-five years old.

Broke.

Divorced twice.

With two children.

Those facts felt heavy that night, like labels stitched too tightly to my skin.

When my friend arrived, I finally said out loud what I'd been holding in: my fear of being seen, my uncertainty, my worry that I wouldn't belong anywhere anymore. I told him I wasn't sure I knew how to do this—how to go out, how to be social, how to pretend my world hadn't already collapsed twice.

He smiled gently and said, "You're going to be fine."

Then he added, "You're twenty-five. You're far too young to think your life is over."

He reminded me that I had grown up in this town—that I had gone to school with most of the people we might see. And then, with a kindness that steadied me more than he probably realized, he said, "Don't worry. I'll be right there beside you."

That was all I needed.

Not confidence.

Not certainty.

Just someone willing to stand next to me while I took one small step back into the world.

And sometimes, when we step forward without expectation, trusting our prayers will be answered, life meets us quietly—not with answers, but with possibility.

That night of dancing I met a man with the most beautiful blue eyes.

I remember standing there, caught off guard—surprised by how quickly warmth moved through me. There was lightness. A sense of ease. And underneath it all, fear. The kind that shows up when something feels right and risky at the same time.

My first thought wasn't excitement.

It was caution.

God is testing me, I told myself. *I cannot—and will not—feel this way so soon.*

So I did what I knew how to do when something stirred too much hope. I ran.

But the question didn't leave me. As my friend and I drove home, it followed quietly in the space between us: *What would need to change in me to create the relationship I truly wanted?*

For the first time, the question wasn't about choosing the right person. It was about becoming the right partner—to myself.

Once again, counseling became my guide.

My counselor offered a truth that reshaped everything: Until you love yourself, it will be difficult to truly love another.

I resisted at first. I believed love was something I could give regardless of how I felt about myself. I thought effort, sacrifice, and endurance were enough.

Healing taught me otherwise.

I began to understand that dignity starts within—that self-worth is not something a relationship gives us, but something we bring with us. Without it, love slowly turns into fear, self-abandonment, and survival.

Slowly, I learned to value myself—not only as a mother, not only as a survivor, but as a whole person. I rebuilt stability. Confidence. Self-trust.

And I made a promise to myself—one rooted in dignity:

Even if marriage never happened again, I would not abandon myself. I would be a strong, loving mother. I would raise confident children. And I would live from worth, not fear.

That promise changed everything.

Third Time's the Charm

That man I met dancing became my husband.

For thirty-four years, we've built a marriage rooted not in perfection but in respect.

Marriage isn't about getting it right all the time.

It's about choosing each other again and again.

Love is an action.

Listening. Repairing. Forgiving. Growing.

Counseling saved our marriage more than once. And I am grateful for every step, even the painful ones, because they shaped the partnership I cherish today.

Sometimes, it really is true:

Third time's the charm.

But charm has nothing to do with ease.

What we built was not luck—it was presence, intention, and the willingness to keep choosing each other through seasons of change.

Over time, I learned that marriage does not thrive on grand gestures alone. It survives—and deepens—through everyday moments of attention. Through showing up. Through noticing who is standing in front of you now, not who they used to be.

Marriage, at its heart, is a practice of presence.

Intentional time strengthens connection. With your partner, remember who you were before responsibilities took over. Dream together. Talk beyond logistics.

Presence builds trust.

Your marriage matters.

Your well-being matters.

Asking for help is not weakness.

It is wisdom.

When times were turbulent in our relationship, we had this mantra: "We are an effective team."

Love Languages and Everyday Translation

One of the most practical tools we learned was understanding love languages:

- Quality Time
- Gifts
- Acts of Service
- Physical Touch
- Words of Affirmation

Sometimes love is present—it's just not landing.

Marriage isn't about giving equally. It's about giving intentionally. Marriage isn't proven by the absence of conflict. It's proven by the willingness to repair, return, and choose love—with respect intact.

Wisdom Moment

Marriage is not about finding the right person. It's about becoming partners.

Helping each other to be their best selves. Love grows through presence, honesty, and the choice to return to each other, again and again.

A Pause for Reflection

If you were sitting across from me,

I'd invite you to take a breath.

Marriage is personal. It stirs memory, longing, and truth.

There is no right way to hold what's come up

—only an honest one.

Marriage—Your Reflective Journey

1. Partnership and Presence

Feels like: Connection, distance, effort

Reveals: How present you are with one another beyond

roles and routines

- When do I feel most connected to my partner?
- When do I feel the most distant?
- What helps me return to presence rather than avoidance?

2. Conflict and Repair

Feels like: Tension, defensiveness, vulnerability

Reveals: How conflict is handled and healed

- How do I typically respond when conflict arises?
- What helps me move from reaction to repair?
- Where might an honest conversation bring relief or clarity?

3. Self-Worth Within Relationship

Feels like: Confidence, insecurity, longing

Reveals: How well you stay anchored in yourself while loving another

- Where do I feel most secure in who I am within my marriage?
- Where do I lose myself or shrink?
- What would it look like to honor both my needs and the relationship?

4. Commitment and Choice

Feels like: Dedication, fatigue, devotion

Reveals: Marriage as an ongoing, conscious choice

- What does choosing my partner look like today—not just in the past?
- How have we grown together through challenge?
- What kind of marriage am I committed to creating now?

Wisdom to Carry Forward

- Marriage is a living, evolving partnership.
- Emotional literacy protects intimacy.
- Resentment grows where truth is avoided.
- Healthy love is built on respect, not control.
- Healing yourself strengthens relationships.
- Counseling is wisdom, not failure.
- One-on-one time builds connection.
- Love languages help love land.
- Steady love can be sacred.

A GROUNDING WORD

"Above all, love each other deeply,
because love covers over a multitude of sins."
—1 Peter 4:8

Closing Blessing

May you release the fairy tale and
embrace the deeper work of love.
May courage guide your conversations
and tenderness soften your hearts.
May respect remain—even in disagreement.
And may the love you build be steady enough to weather storms
and gentle enough to keep your hearts open.

Journey Ten

THE WISDOM OF FAMILY

"Family is not an important thing, it's everything."
—Michael J. Fox

Family Togetherness: A Tradition of Joy and Unity

EVERY RING OF WISDOM HAS A PLACE WHERE BELONGING IS FIRST LEARNED. In this journey, that place is family.

The Wisdom of Family is the chapter that inspired this entire book. It carries the legacy of those who came before me—the place where God planted my earliest lessons through my grandparents' hands, my parents' choices, and the generations whose stories still echo in my heart.

Writing this chapter felt like honoring those roots and recognizing how love and imperfection together shaped my purpose. This is the foundation of my wisdom journey—the part of the book that feels most like home.

My belief in family togetherness began early. One of my grandmothers had thirteen brothers and sisters, which meant our family was expansive and ever present—a close-knit community full of laughter, connection, and shared life.

Summers were especially magical. I spent them with my Grandmother Helena and Grandpa Dewitt, surrounded by aunts, uncles, cousins, and friends who felt like family. Those weeks were woven with simple joys: cooking and baking together, picking berries from sun-dappled bushes, milking cows in the quiet of early morning, riding horses through rolling fields.

With my cousins, hours passed laughing in creeks and exploring the woods that wrapped around my grandmother's home. Life felt wide, safe, and shared.

The highlight of each year was our annual weeklong family gathering—a tradition rooted in joy and unity. We gathered at a sprawling campsite tucked among towering trees, serenaded by the steady music of nature. Days were spent sharing meals, playing endless games, and enjoying the sacred simplicity of being together.

And then there was the nightly campfire.

As the sky darkened and stars appeared, we gathered in a circle of old and young faces, warmed by the fire's glow. Uncle George cradled his guitar, leading us in song. The melodies were simple, but the sound of our voices blending under the open sky felt almost holy.

The adults shared stories from their youth, laughter mixing with the crackle of the flames. We kids huddled nearby, talking in the bubbling stream of dreams only children can create.

Time slowed.

Those moments shaped me. They became threads woven into the fabric of my childhood—love, security, strength, and playfulness. Around that campfire, wisdom was passed down—not through lectures, but through laughter, presence, and the steady glow of togetherness. The flames seemed like they were dancing in the center of the circle, reminding me that belonging is something you feel, not explain.

And yet, no fire stays exactly the same.

Family: A Dynamic Adventure

As I grew older, I learned that family does not remain frozen in those golden moments. The circle widens. The fire goes out. Seasons change.

Family, to me, is an adventure—full of peaks and valleys, unexpected turns, and moments that shape us in ways we don't see until later. Family is not one-size-fits-all.

Some families are formed by birth. Some by marriage. Some through adoption, fostering, or the many modern ways children come into our lives. And some of the strongest family bonds are chosen—built not by blood, but by loyalty, love, and shared experience.

Whatever shape your family takes, what matters most is this:

Who shows up.

Who stays.

Who helps you become more of who you truly are.

Family takes patience. It takes understanding. And sometimes, it asks a brave question: *How am I showing up for my family—right now? What am I modeling?*

We often ask these questions hoping for reassurance. But sometimes, life answers them through change we didn't choose—through moments that test what we thought was stable and expose what was fragile beneath the surface.

Fractured Foundations: When Family Changes

Even families built on warmth and tradition can fracture.

The disruption of my parents' divorce ushered in a new chapter—one where the stability I believed was permanent unraveled quickly. One moment, we were a family. The next, my parents announced they were done.

My father moved out, and with him went the familiar rhythm of home. The lively hum of four voices became an unsettling quiet. Weekends turned into scheduled visits. Goodbyes carried a weight I didn't yet have language for.

As a teenager, I carried the fallout in my body. I often say I became the proud owner of a car called anger—painted with resentment, dented with sadness, fueled by blame.

The storybook family I once knew had changed.
And so had I.

Redefining Family: Choosing New Values

It wasn't until counseling in my early twenties that I learned something essential: Everyone carries their own definition of *family*.

What you witness—or endure—often becomes your starting point, until you pause long enough to decide what you want to keep and what you're ready to release.

I realized I had to rewrite my story.

I had to let go of perfection—because no family and no person is perfect. And I had to build a new foundation rooted in love, compassion, dignity, communication, and growth.

Family life is a tapestry of moods and emotions—woven together through joy, conflict, loss, and repair. Acceptance doesn't mean pretending. It means seeing clearly and choosing how you want to live within what is real.

And eventually, clarity asks something more of us—not just to understand where we came from, but to decide what continues and what ends with us.

Breaking the Generational Cycle

At some point in every family, one person chooses to break the cycles of behaviors and habits that erode relationships. I knew I was going to be that person—for the generations ahead of me.

To feel instead of freeze.

To speak instead of being silent.

To heal instead of passing wounds forward.

Breaking generational patterns is not rejection.

It is discernment.

It honors what once protected us while choosing what will heal us now.

We don't break cycles because our families failed us.

We break them because we love deeply enough to want something healthier to continue.

In my thirties, I attended a conference on generational patterns—and I was captivated by what I heard. For the first time, I was given language and understanding for something I had felt my entire life but could never quite name.

From that day forward, I began seeking ways to understand my own patterns—and, more importantly, how to interrupt the ones that no longer served me or my family.

Not because I was ashamed of where I came from.

Quite the opposite.

I hold deep respect for the generations before me. Without their modeling—their strengths and their struggles—I would not have felt the impact clearly enough to want something different. Awareness is often born from contrast. We recognize what needs to change because we have lived inside what was.

What I came to understand is this:

If we are not willing to look honestly at how we are showing up, we will continue to re-create what feels familiar—even when it hurts.

Generational patterns do not repeat because we want them to. They repeat because they are unexamined.

As I began to see this, I noticed how my responses, reactions, boundaries—and my silence—were shaping the relationships I was experiencing. That realization was humbling.

And it was empowering.

Because once you can see the pattern, you can choose differently.

Breaking generational shackles is not about blame.

It is about responsibility.

It is the moment you recognize that healing does not dishonor the past—it builds upon it. It is how we honor those who came before us while choosing a healthier legacy for those who come after.

That choice—made one conversation, one boundary, one pause at a time—is how the Ring of Wisdom stays alive.

The fire remains.

But the way we gather around it begins to change.

To support this work, I sought out practical, evidence-based tools that could reach beneath conscious thought—where generational patterns often live. I attended a weekend certification in Neuro-Linguistic Programming (NLP), where I was introduced to techniques such as Timeline Therapy, reframing, Meta-Model questioning, and swish patterns.

What fascinated me most was how these tools address subconscious beliefs and emotional responses that are often inherited, unexamined, and quietly shaping our relationships.

Rather than endlessly retelling old stories, this work allowed me to identify where patterns began, reframe the meaning attached to them, and release what no longer belonged to me. It created space to rewrite my personal narrative—not out of shame for where I came from, but out of respect for what I wanted to pass forward.

Alongside this, I experienced EMDR (Eye Movement Desensitization and Reprocessing), a highly effective, evidence-based therapy designed to help the brain reprocess traumatic memories. Through bilateral stimulation, memories that once carried a heavy emotional charge began to soften and integrate. What had felt stuck in my body finally found movement and resolution.

Together, these approaches changed my way of being.

Timeline work, in particular, offered insight into my past that logic alone could never reach. And with that understanding came freedom. For the past five years, this wisdom has guided my choices—helping me take paths I once would have avoided and lovingly say no to ones I would have followed out of habit or fear.

This work did not disconnect me from my family story.

It grounded me in it.

And from that place of awareness, I learned how generational cycles truly end—not by rejecting the past, but by understanding it deeply enough to choose differently and lean on what was influential.

Healing invited me to become that person.

I learned to:

- communicate honestly
- regulate emotions with compassion
- build boundaries that protect dignity
- forgive without abandoning myself
- stop carrying what was never mine
- soften without losing strength
- trust in love again

Wisdom Moment

Family gives us our roots, but not our limits.

The wisdom is in honoring where we come from while becoming who we're meant to be.

A Pause for Reflection

Before moving on, take a breath.

Let the memories—both tender and tenderized

—settle in your body.

Notice what feels warm. Notice what still aches.

This is not about judgment. It is about awareness.

Family—Your Reflective Journey

1. Belonging and Togetherness

Feels like: Warmth, nostalgia, safety

Reveals: Where connection has shaped your sense of home

- When have I felt most connected and at ease within family?

- What moments or traditions still live warmly in my body?

- How do I experience belonging today—who or what provides it?

2. Fracture and Change

Feels like: Loss, confusion, grief

Reveals: How disruption has influenced your emotional patterns

- What family change or rupture shaped me most?
- What emotions did I carry without language at the time?
- How has that experience influenced the way I relate today?

3. Choice and Redefinition

Feels like: Clarity, resolve, uncertainty

Reveals: Your power to choose what family means now

- What values do I want to carry forward from my family of origin?
- What patterns am I ready to release?
- How am I redefining family in ways that honor my truth?

4. Legacy and Healing

Feels like: Responsibility, hope, steadiness

Reveals: The legacy you are shaping through awareness and care

- Where am I interrupting generational patterns?
- How do I model dignity, communication, and love?
- What legacy do I want my presence to leave behind?

Wisdom to Carry Forward

- Family can be loving, complicated, and evolving all at once.
- Togetherness is built through presence, not perfection.
- Patterns are powerful—but not permanent.
- Healing begins when one person interrupts the cycle.
- Boundaries protect love and dignity.
- Grace and truth can coexist.
- Your family shaped you—but doesn't have to define you.
- You can honor where you came from while choosing who you become.

A GROUNDING WORD

"Love is patient, love is kind. It does not envy,
it does not boast, it is not proud."
—1 Corinthians 13:4

Closing Blessing

Family gives us our first emotional language, our earliest patterns,
and some of our deepest lessons.
As this chapter closes, may you feel the echo of your own story—
its joys, fractures, and truths—settling gently within you.
May you keep what nourishes you.
May you release what no longer belongs to you.
May you build family—by blood, by choice, or by both—that
allows you to feel safe, seen, and loved.
And may dignity be the thread that holds it all.

Journey Eleven

THE WISDOM OF RAISING CHILDREN

"The beauty of children is in their adaptation. We must nurture their spirit and never put limits on their potential; the plan we have for them may be the very thing that limits them. Never forget they are whole as they are—we are the ones who have to learn to listen differently."
—Dana Hall

The Gift of Raising Children

EVERY RING OF WISDOM HAS A PLACE WHERE LOVE ASKS MORE OF US THAN WE THINK WE CAN GIVE.

In this journey, that place is parenting.

Moms, you are truly special people. And dads, you are too.

I always knew I wanted to be a mother. Growing up in a big family, I felt like I carried an old soul—one that longed for marriage, children, and a home filled with warmth and laughter. Motherhood wasn't a phase or a preference for me; it was a calling I felt long before I held my first child.

Parenting is one of the most important roles in the world—just as essential as building bridges, designing homes, or practicing medicine. Why? Because parents raise the people who go on to do all of that. You are shaping the bridge builders, the artists, the nurses, the leaders, the teachers, the service providers, the healers, and the ones who will someday raise families of their own.

You teach.

You guide.

You nurture.

You love—again and again.

Parenthood doesn't just *require* wisdom.

It *creates* it.

Born with a Story All Their Own

Raising children begins long before they take their first breath.

Each child arrives with their own spirit, temperament, and story already unfolding—and from the moment they are placed in our arms, they begin shaping us as much as we shape them.

My husband and I are blessed with four children—two boys and two girls—each arriving in their own unforgettable way.

We chose not to learn the gender ahead of time. After nine months of waiting, I wanted the surprise to meet us at the finish line.

Christian, my firstborn, arrived via scheduled cesarean—calm and intentional, ushering me into the breathtaking love of motherhood. Elizabeth arrived a month early—decisive, determined, and eager to make her entrance.

Brian took his time, arriving two weeks late, as if carefully deciding when the moment was right.

And then there was Alicia—our whirlwind—arriving on her due date so quickly we barely made it to the hospital.

Each birth carried its own lesson in patience, surrender, and awe.

As the years passed, the little hands that once reached for mine began reaching for the world. I had to learn a new wisdom—the wisdom of loosening my grip without losing my love.

The Season of Parenting Years

Parenting is not one journey—it is many.

The early years taught me presence and patience. Children feel truth long before they understand words, and my emotional state mattered more than any lesson I tried to teach.

The middle years invited curiosity. Listening beneath behavior. Guiding without suffocating.

The teenage years required steadiness. Their emotions often felt bigger than mine, and I learned that teens don't need a perfect parent—they need a regulated one.

And the adult years revealed the deepest wisdom of all:

Love evolves.

Stepping back becomes devotion.

Trust replaces control.

Parenting is not about shaping a child into who we want them to be. It is about becoming the person they need—while trusting who God designed them to become.

Guiding with Love, Growing with Time

Motherhood brought constant questions:

Am I doing this right?

Will they love God?

How do I teach dignity, resilience, and kindness?

How do I protect without controlling?

And those questions don't disappear.

They evolve.

Over time, you begin to see the seeds you planted.

A moment of compassion.

A boundary held with integrity.

A voice used to protect another.

And something inside you softens.

Maybe—just maybe—I did something right.

Parenting isn't about perfection.

It's about presence.

And unconditional love is dignity in action.

But presence doesn't mean ease.

And dignity doesn't remove weight.

When love is lived day after day—without pause, without certainty— it begins to carry an emotional cost that must be acknowledged.

That is where the next wisdom lives.

The Emotional Load of Parenting

Parenthood is an emotional marathon.

Joy, pride, anxiety, guilt, frustration, fear—sometimes all in one day.

I grew up in a home where emotions weren't named—not out of neglect, but survival. My parents were raised by parents shaped by the Great Depression, war, and scarcity. They endured. They provided. They kept going. When we learn to name feelings, pause before reacting, repair when we miss the mark, and treat emotions as information—not threats—we give our children tools they will carry for life.

And we must remember:

You cannot pour from an empty cup.

The Advice That Changed Everything

At twenty-six, preparing to remarry with two children, I sat across from a counselor who said something that stopped me cold:

"Taking care of a family starts with: First, it's Sandy. Then it's Scott. Then it's the children."

I resisted.

My children didn't come first?

She gently explained that one day, children grow and leave—and if you haven't nurtured yourself or your partnership, you may not recognize who remains.

That moment reframed everything.

Motherhood isn't about disappearing.

It's about balance.

Love with boundaries.

Dignity for yourself and those you love.

Parenting Across Seasons

There are seasons where children need structure.

Others where they need listening.

And later, where they need trust.

In the adult years, our role shifts from teaching to witnessing.

One of the most powerful questions we can ask is:

"Would you like my wisdom or my listening?"

And if the answer is no, we honor it.

That respect builds confidence, responsibility, and trust.

Becoming a Grandmother

While finishing this chapter, I stepped into a new season—grandmotherhood.

Watching my daughter become a mother felt like time folding in on itself.

This season invited me to listen more.

Observe more.

Hold space instead of solutions.

And dignity guided me through this fragile transition.

One truth matters deeply:

Never use access to a grandchild as control.

This season requires tenderness, communication, and grace—for everyone.

Wisdom Moment

Raising children is not about shaping who they should be. It's about guiding who they already are becoming.

A Pause for Reflection

Before moving on, smile—and remember:

Motherhood never came with a handbook.

You did the best you could with what you knew at the time.

Let that be enough for this moment.

Raising Children—Your Reflective Journey

1. When Your Child Becomes Their Own Person

Feels like: Pride mixed with surrender

Reveals: Your role is shifting

- Where do I need to honor who my child truly is?

- What expectations am I holding too tightly?

- How can I trust their becoming?

2. When Emotions Run High

Feels like: Overwhelm or urgency

Reveals: A need for regulation, not fixing

- How do I respond to big emotions?
- What helps me stay grounded?
- What repair seems needed right now?

3. When Letting Go Is Required

Feels like: Bittersweet pride

Reveals: Love is evolving

- Where am I being invited to step back?
- What does trust look like here?
- How can I support without controlling?

4. When You Need Care Too

Feels like: Exhaustion or resentment

Reveals: Your needs matter

- What part of me needs attention?
- Where do I need rest or support?
- What boundary would serve everyone?

Wisdom to Carry Forward

- Parenting is a sacred classroom where wisdom is lived.
- Children arrive whole; our role is to unfold, not mold.
- Each season of life invites a different form of love.
- Your nervous system teaches theirs.
- Emotional literacy turns conflict into connection.
- Boundaries are love in action.
- Your well-being is part of your child's foundation.
- Presence creates belonging.
- Grandparenthood is love without pressure.
- Dignity remains the north star.

A GROUNDING WORD

"Children are a gift from the Lord, a reward from Him."
—Psalm 127:3

Closing Blessing

Raising children invites us into courage, patience, surrender, and fierce love. There was no handbook. You did the best you could.
May you trust the wisdom you've earned.
May you lead with dignity.
May repair come easier than shame.
And may love—steady, brave, and present—continue to shape every generation that follows.

Journey Twelve

THE WISDOM OF RAISING A CHILD WITH SPECIAL NEEDS

"I may not have gone where I intended to go,
but I think I have ended up where I needed to be."
—Douglas Adams

At the Heart of Special-Needs Parenting

EVERY RING OF WISDOM HAS A PLACE WHERE LOVE IS REFINED—NOT IN THEORY, BUT IN REAL TIME.

In this journey, that place is *raising a child with special needs.*

This wisdom lives close to the center of the Ring, because it asks for everything at once: presence, patience, advocacy, surrender, and a fierce kind of love that keeps showing up—even when you're exhausted, unsure, or afraid.

Parenting always stretches us. But parenting a child with special needs stretches *the whole family system*—your marriage, your nervous system, your schedule, your finances, your faith, and your identity. It introduces you to a world you never asked to navigate, and it asks you to become strong in ways you didn't know you could.

And yet it also brings a kind of sacred clarity.

Because this journey teaches something the Ring returns to again and again: Your child is not a problem to solve—your child is a person to honor.

Here, wisdom is carried through appointments, therapy plans, school meetings, surgeries, and quiet nights when your mind won't stop racing. It is carried in the smallest victories and the hardest conversations. It is carried in the steady decision to advocate without losing your tenderness—and to protect dignity without losing your heart.

This chapter is about what happens when life doesn't go according to plan...and love becomes both the path *and* the strength to walk it.

And for me, that journey began with two words that changed everything:

It's a Boy

On September 9, 1987, I gave birth to my first child—a little boy we named Christian.

My whole world shifted in an instant.

After months of anticipation and a scheduled cesarean section—Christian had been breech, and the doctors felt it was the safest option—I heard his first cry. It was powerful and raw, and it wrapped itself around my heart forever. I was holding the greatest gift I had ever received.

I was a young mother, but I knew—deep in my soul—that I was meant for this.

In that moment, I made a silent promise.

To love him.

To protect him.

To show up—no matter what life brought.

Forever.

I watched him grow with pride, celebrating every milestone, no matter how big or small. His determination showed early. He pulled himself up using furniture, shuffled along the couch, gripping whatever he could with sheer willpower. And when he managed a few steps, his face lit up like he had conquered the world.

And still...deep down, I knew.

Something wasn't quite right.

A quiet whisper of doubt had been growing inside me for months. At his six-month checkup, the doctor reassured me: *Children develop at their own pace.* I wanted to believe that.

But my instincts wouldn't let it go.

So I picked up the phone and made an appointment with another doctor.

The Moment Time Stood Still

Sitting in the doctor's office, I held Christian in my lap, running my fingers through his soft hair as we waited. He babbled and pointed at the colorful posters on the wall—curious, alive, completely himself.

The doctor examined him, observed his movement, asked questions, and took notes.

Then he paused.

"I'd like to send you to a neurologist. I believe he may have cerebral palsy. Mild—but he has classic signs."

Time stopped.

The doctor kept talking, but his voice felt muffled, as if I'd been placed inside a snow globe—everything swirling in slow motion.

Cerebral palsy.

The words echoed—heavy, unfamiliar, suddenly defining a reality I hadn't prepared for.

What does this mean?

What will his future look like?

Will he be okay?

My mind shut down.

How would I take care of a child with special needs?

How would I protect him?

And if I'm honest, one of my first fears was how the world would look at us.

I remembered how children with differences were treated when I was young—the stares in grocery stores. The whispers. The judgment.

Stares I'm ashamed to admit I had once participated in.

And suddenly, I feared that same cruelty for my child.

No one prepares you for a moment like this—when the life you thought you were stepping into shifts with a single sentence.

And yet, even in the shock, one truth rose quietly inside me:

He was still the same child I loved the day before the diagnosis.

I held him tighter.

As we stepped into the hallway, his little voice carried on—joyful, curious, untouched by the heaviness settling in my chest.

The diagnosis changed my world.

It did not change him.

And in that contrast, something steadied me.

I didn't know what the road ahead would look like.

But I knew I had to take the next step.

Not with certainty—but with courage.

The Journey of Advocacy

Cerebral palsy wasn't something I expected, and at first, I felt completely unprepared.

But I learned quickly that love and intuition are more powerful than any medical term.

Advocacy didn't arrive all at once. It unfolded through small, determined moments:

- learning language I never wanted to know
- holding my son through appointments and therapies
- asking questions I didn't yet know how to form
- pushing—gently and firmly—for the support he needed

And in the middle of it all, a truth anchored me:

No one knows your child like you do.

Nothing prepares you for the moment your world shifts. Sometimes it comes through a diagnosis. Sometimes through an accident. Suddenly, life is different.

Your child's life is different.

At first, it can feel like a flood—worry, sadness, disbelief, even grief.

Not grief because your child is gone.

Grief because you are releasing the path you once imagined.

And still, within the uncertainty, something new begins to form.

A different kind of vision.

A different definition of strength.

Acceptance, I learned, has many timelines.

And while I was moving into action, someone else in our home was standing still.

That's where the next chapter began.

Not in paperwork.

Not in plans.

But inside our marriage.

From Denial to Acceptance

When Christian was diagnosed, I knew we were stepping into something different.

What I wasn't prepared for was how my husband responded.

The denial.

The resistance.

The quiet, devastating insistence: *This isn't possible.*

It shattered me.

While I was drowning in fear and uncertainty, I assumed we would face it together.

Instead, he pulled away—unable, perhaps unwilling, to accept that our child's life, and our life, would not follow the script we'd imagined.

Denial is a form of grief.

A powerful kind of self-protection.

In those early days, it felt like we were living in two different worlds:

Me—trying to understand.

Him—trying to reject.

And I felt alone in a way I never expected.

Still, I knew one thing:

Our son deserved love, support, and possibility—not limitation.

And I was determined to give him that.

Acceptance didn't arrive all at once.

It came in pieces.

In Christian's full-body laughter.

In his smile that was so big

In his soft blue eyes with the longest eyelashes I had ever seen

In the pride on his face when he mastered something new.

In the resilience he showed, day after day.

Acceptance wasn't surrender.

It was expansion.

Of my heart.

Of my strength.

Of my understanding of what parenting truly meant.

Acceptance, I learned, is not a moment.

It's a practice.

Acceptance in the Journey

Life moves differently when you're raising a child with special needs.

There's more to process.

More to prepare for.

More to hold.

Some days feel like progress.

Other days, you feel frozen—wondering if you're doing enough. If you *are* enough.

Acceptance isn't about fixing your child.

It's about understanding them.

Meeting them where they are.

Walking beside them at their pace.

And in doing that, you begin to see a different kind of beauty.

A life not measured by comparison—

but by resilience, patience, and love.

What has always amazed me is how naturally children accept life as it is.

They see people before labels.

They meet difference with curiosity, not judgment.

Watching my other children grow alongside Christian—learning from him, loving him—filled me with gratitude.

This journey didn't just shape me.

It shaped our entire family.

Wisdom Shared Through Siblings

Raising a child with special needs transforms siblings too.

Elizabeth, even as a toddler, became a protector—watchful, compassionate, deeply loyal.

Brian learned patience and unconditional love in the quietest ways—sitting beside Christian for hours, sharing a language without words.

Alicia brought laughter, playfulness, and adaptability—absorbing resilience through rhythm rather than explanation.

These are gifts no parenting book can teach.

Siblings become softer and stronger at the same time.

And that bond becomes a living thread in the family's Ring of Wisdom.

Navigating the System Without Losing Yourself

No one prepares you for the system.

The acronyms.

The paperwork.

The meetings where decisions feel rushed and assumptions feel heavy.

Some days you leave hopeful.

Other days you cry in the car before driving home.

Over time, you learn how to speak up.

How to pause.

How to say, *I need more time.*

And you learn this truth in your bones:

You are your child's most important advocate.

Not because you know everything—but because you know *them.*

The Wisdom of Dignity

Every child is born with dignity.

Diagnosis or no diagnosis.

Ability or disability.

Their dignity is whole.

And so is yours.

Before I had the language for dignity, I lived it.

I refused to let my child be reduced to charts, timelines, or assumptions.

Advocating with dignity changed everything.

I stopped apologizing.

I stopped shrinking.

I stopped hoping to be heard—and started expecting partnership.

We weren't asking for special treatment.

We were asking for fair treatment.

And dignity turned toward me, too.

Reminding me:

I am learning.

I am growing.

I deserve grace.

And then another truth emerged—quietly, but unmistakably.

This journey was never meant to be walked alone.

Even the strongest love needs witnesses.

Even the most devoted parents need support.

And even when dignity holds us upright, isolation can still creep in.

That is when this wisdom became clear:

You Are Not Alone

This journey can feel isolating.
The long nights.
The unanswered questions.
The quiet fear.
But there are others walking it too.
Let people stand with you.
Not because you are weak—
but because being supported makes you stronger.

The Unexpected Gifts

This path carries gifts you don't expect:
- patience
- perspective
- joy in small victories
- love that deepens beyond language

They don't erase the hard moments.
But they soften them.

Wisdom Moment

Sometimes the bravest love isn't loud.
It's the steady decision to show up again today—
eyes open, heart willing, dignity intact.

A Pause for Reflection

Take a moment.

Let the weight of this journey—the love, the fear, the courage, the exhaustion—settle gently in your body.

This is not about getting it right. It is about honoring what you have carried.

You are allowed to reflect without fixing.

You are allowed to feel without explaining.

Raising a Child with Special Needs— Your Reflective Journey

1. The Moment Everything Changed

Feels like: Shock, fear, protective instinct

Reveals: The instant life shifted—and a new kind of strength emerged

- What moment first signaled to me that my child's path would be different?
- What emotions rose first—and which ones surprised me?
- What helped me take the next step when I didn't feel ready?

2. Grief, Acceptance, and Letting Go

Feels like: Sadness, guilt, tenderness

Reveals: Releasing imagined futures and meeting what is real

- What expectations did I have to grieve or redefine?
- How has acceptance shown up in layers rather than all at once?
- What has softened in me over time?

3. Advocacy and Inner Strength

Feels like: Determination, exhaustion, empowerment

Reveals: The courage to speak, stand, and persist

- When did I realize I had to become my child's advocate?
- Where have I found strength I didn't know I had?
- What advocacy moment am I quietly proud of?

4. Love, Dignity, and Identity

Feels like: Depth, connection, clarity

Reveals: Love that is rooted in presence, not performance

- How has this journey reshaped the way I understand love?
- In what ways have I learned to honor my child's dignity—and my own?
- Who am I becoming through this path?

Wisdom to Carry Forward

- Your child is whole—not a diagnosis to manage, but a human to know.
- Advocacy is love in motion; your voice matters more than you realize.
- Grief and gratitude can coexist without canceling each other out.
- Acceptance is not surrender—it is an expansion of the heart.
- Dignity belongs to your child and to you, in every room you enter.

A GROUNDING WORD

"Before I formed you in the womb I knew you,
before you were born I set you apart"
—Jeremiah 1:5

Closing Blessing

May you trust your instincts.
May you release comparison.
May you receive support without guilt.
May you remember:
You are not alone.
And may the Ring of Wisdom hold you—
just as you have held your child—
with strength, patience, and enduring love.

Journey Thirteen

THE WISDOM OF DIVORCE

"Although the world is full of suffering,
it is also full of the overcoming of it."
—Helen Keller

The Threshold in the Ring: When the Ground Shifts

EVERY RING OF WISDOM HAS A PLACE WHERE THE GROUND BENEATH US CHANGES.

In this journey, that place is divorce.

Divorce is not only the ending of a marriage.

It is the breaking of an assumed future.

A rupture in safety.

A reorganization of identity, belonging, and trust.

For many of us, the wisdom of divorce begins long before we ever choose it—or survive it ourselves.

Sometimes, it begins when we are still children.

The Journey of Divorce

In my eleven-year-old mind, life felt simple and sweet. My childhood seemed like a storybook—full of laughter, warmth, and a sense of safety I trusted without question. My parents were my heroes: devoted, hardworking, united. From the outside, our family looked whole. They stood together—a united front. To me, their bond wasn't just built on ambition, but on love.

I believed we were some of the lucky ones.

I never saw cracks in their foundation.

Never questioned the safety of the world they had created for us.

I never imagined that world could fracture so suddenly.

The first tremor didn't arrive gently.

There was no careful buildup, no soft preparation.

It came the way real tremors do—sudden, disorienting, and without mercy.

I had just flown home from a summer vacation in Florida with my cousins. Back then, families could meet you right at the gate. I remember spotting my mother and brother waiting for me—familiar faces I couldn't wait to run toward.

Before I could reach them, before I could even speak, my brother blurted out the words that split my world open:

"Mom and Dad are getting a divorce."

The air left the terminal.

The words crashed over me like a tidal wave, washing away the warmth, the laughter, the certainty I had always known. My eleven-year-old mind couldn't make sense of them. I tried desperately to hold on to the picture of who we were, a family that worked, that loved, that lasted.

But that picture was already fading.

The word *divorce* hung in the air—thick, heavy, suffocating. Tears streamed down my face as my body stiffened in shock. My heart raced while my mind filled with questions too big to speak. The life I believed was unbreakable was unraveling in front of me.

I didn't have words for what I was experiencing at the time. Now I know it was anguish.

And I was standing right in the middle of it—lost, afraid, and suddenly unsure of the world I had trusted without question.

I didn't know where to put it, only that everything felt different now.

The car ride home felt like crossing into a life I didn't recognize. I sat in the back seat, staring out the window as familiar roads blurred past, suddenly belonging to someone else's story.

No one spoke.

The silence was heavy and dense, almost loud. I kept waiting for someone to say something that would make it less terrifying. Nothing came.

By the time we pulled into the driveway, the girl who had stepped off the airplane carefree and bright now felt like she had been left somewhere between the airport and home.

The Official Sit-Down

A few days later, the second tremor arrived.

My parents sat my brother and me down in the living room—a space that once held birthday parties, Christmas mornings, and ordinary family moments. That day, the air felt different. Still. Weighted.

"We're getting a divorce."

Hearing it from them didn't soften the blow.

It made it final.

Tears came before I could stop them. Fear, disbelief, grief, confusion, and anger collided inside my eleven-year-old body. I searched their faces for reassurance, something to hold on to, but there were no words that could make it untrue.

The world I trusted shifted again.

Divorce Creates Uncertainty

After the words were spoken, silence took over.

I needed someone, anyone, to say this was a misunderstanding. To promise that everything would be okay. But no one did. The quiet pressed in, heavy and unrelenting, crushing the fragile hope I tried to cling to.

It felt like we were all holding our breath, unsure how to move inside the gravity of what had just been said. The unknown settled in my chest like a stone.

My brother and I stumbled into this new reality together, trying to find footing in a landscape that had shifted overnight. The house looked the same, but it no longer felt like home. Everything familiar now carried an edge.

Even the walls seemed to mourn with us.

This wasn't just a change in our family—it was a rupture in the foundation of our lives. And we were left to navigate it one careful, uncertain step at a time.

The Sadness of Divorce

In the days that followed, the confusion deepened.

Sadness settled into my body like a low ache. Grief for what had been and fear for what was now. Life, once steady and predictable, had become fragile and unfamiliar.

My mother stayed busy. She cleaned, folded, refolded and moved through the house like a ghost. Physically present, emotionally somewhere far away. I wanted to ask her everything: *Why is this happening? What will happen to us?* But fear kept me silent. I wasn't ready for answers that might hurt more than the questions.

My brother and I whispered to each other, piecing together our own understanding of something none of us knew how to explain.

We clung to each other, trying to make sense of a puzzle with too many missing pieces.

Eventually, one truth settled in:

My father wasn't coming back.

And with that realization, something precious was lost, not just a parent under the same roof, but the sense of safety I would spend years trying to rebuild.

When Grief Hardens into Anger

As the months passed, sadness didn't fade.

It hardened.

Grief, when it has nowhere to go, sharpens into something more combustible.

For me, that something was anger.

My parents were moving on. Finding other people, building new lives, while I was still standing in the wreckage, trying to understand what had happened. Their worlds seemed to move forward quickly. Mine felt frozen in shock.

They were finding people to soothe *their* emptiness.

Mine was still wide-open.

I could not understand how the heartbreak had been so final for us, yet so temporary for them. How the family we had been seemed to dissolve overnight. New lives began forming without my consent, without my readiness, without my voice.

Anger took root.

I hated my dad's girlfriend.

Not because of who she was but because of what she represented: replacement. Proof that what we lost could be substituted, while I was still trying to grasp that it was gone.

When my mother remarried quickly, my body recoiled. I wasn't ready. I was still grieving from the first rupture when another arrived. There was no space to catch my breath, no pause to orient. Just change stacked on top of change.

I learned then that grief doesn't like being rushed.

And when it is, it fights back.

And yet something bright did happen.

My mother was expecting a child.

The news carried a quiet excitement for me. A reason to look forward instead of only back. In a season where so much felt uncertain, the promise of another sibling brought a sense of anticipation and warmth that lifted the heaviness, even if just a little.

When my baby sister was born, something inside me softened.

Holding her felt like holding hope itself, warm, fragile, and real. She didn't erase the pain of what had been lost, but she reminded me that beauty could still emerge from broken places. That love could still arrive, pure and unassuming, even when life no longer looked the way I had imagined it would.

My sister became a gentle reminder that beginnings can coexist with endings, and that the heart, even when bruised, still knows how to open.

But peace didn't follow.

That marriage unraveled. And with it came more loss, more instability, more anger. My mother was carrying her own devastation—loss of marriage, business, financial security, and friendships.

She worked tirelessly to keep us afloat, selling her business, working from home doing hair, then bartending nights to make ends meet.

She was exhausted.

And her unprocessed grief spilled into everything.

We lived inside that emotional crossfire, my sibling and I absorbing more than we could understand, learning to adapt in order to survive.

The only thing I knew to do was pray, and stay out of the way of the wrath happening with my parents and stepparent.

From Survival to Understanding

My nervous system learned vigilance. Silence became safer than questions. Withdrawal felt more protective than expression. I became small—not because I wanted to disappear, but because the chaos felt too big to hold.

I turned inward and learned what it meant to survive each day.

I learned how to read a room before reading myself.

How to keep the peace.

How to step up when needed and disappear when necessary.

But survival and healing are not the same.

I carried an invisible weight into adulthood, wondering if joy could ever exist without anger trailing close behind. Wondering if love was always temporary. Conditional. Fragile.

Eventually, life slowed enough for me to hear my own pain. That became the doorway into understanding.

I learned something important with time:

It takes two to build a marriage.

And it takes two to break one.

The hours became days. The days stretched into months. And somewhere in that long in-between, I learned my role.

I became the one who kept the peace. The one who kept up with the household chores and taking care of my baby sister. While watching my brother withdraw more and more from fun in life.

This was my early training in emotional agility—though I didn't yet have the language to express it. Not the healthy kind rooted in awareness and choice, but the survival kind: adapting quickly, suppressing my own needs, managing other people's emotions so conflict wouldn't erupt.

Outwardly, life kept moving. Inwardly, I felt suspended, waiting for things to make sense, waiting for the ache to settle, waiting for a version of life that didn't feel so sharp at the edges.

As I edged toward adulthood, a quiet question followed me: *Would joy ever arrive without being tangled with anger or pain?* Or was love always accompanied by loss, unpredictability, and the need to stay emotionally alert?

What I didn't know then was that these early adaptations were shaping more than my childhood

They were shaping how I would love.

How I would attach.

How I would choose partners.

How I would stay too long, try too hard, and confuse endurance with commitment.

Before I ever stood at an altar, I had already learned how to brace myself.

The Invisible Backpack

We don't enter adulthood empty-handed.

We carry emotional luggage we never meant to pack, gathered quietly in childhood, shaped by moments we didn't have language for:

- the fear that love and security can disappear without warning
- hypervigilance to other people's emotions
- a longing for steadiness
- a deep need for belonging

For years, I wore that backpack without question, mistaking its weight for normalcy. It traveled with me into relationships, into marriage, into decisions made more from fear of loss than trust in self.

Healing began when I finally paused long enough to set it down and ask:

Does this still belong to me?

Some of it did.

Much of it did not.

And in that moment of discernment, emotional agility began to take on a new meaning, not just adapting to survive, but learning how to feel alive again. To feel, name, and choose differently.

That choice would become essential later when love asked more of me than endurance, and divorce would ask me to separate what I carried from what was never mine to begin with. Finding help to help me release what I needed to let go of and heal from.

The Wisdom That Emerged

Therapy became the doorway to healing

I learned that divorce does not have to mean destruction. That silence wounds. That anger is often grief asking to be heard. That emotional literacy is the bridge between survival and dignity.

Slowly, I stopped demanding perfection from them and from myself. Forgiveness became less about excusing the past and more about releasing myself from its grip.

Divorce shaped me.

But healing refined me.

It taught me clarity.

Resilience.

Emotional strength.

And how to love without losing myself.

Wisdom Moment

Divorce may fracture a family—but it does not fracture your dignity.

Healing begins the moment you choose to accept uncertainty over survival.

A Pause for Reflection

Life asks a lot of us. Before you move on.

Notice what stirred.

Notice what tightened.

Notice what softened.

This is not about blame or fixing.

It is about honoring what shaped you—

and choosing what shapes you next.

Divorce—Your Reflective Journey

1. When the Ground First Shifted

Feels like: Shock, fear, disbelief

Reveals: A moment when safety changed

- What moment first signaled loss or instability for me?

- What did I need then that I didn't receive?

- What would compassion look like now?

2. When Silence Took Over

Feels like: Confusion, loneliness, longing

Reveals: Unspoken grief

- What emotions went unspoken in my family?
- How did silence shape me?
- What wants to be expressed now?

3. When Anger Appeared

Feels like: Heat, defensiveness, reactivity

Reveals: Grief seeking voice

- What anger do I still carry?
- What loss lives underneath it?
- What would release look like?

4. From Survival to Healing

Feels like: Awareness, courage, relief

Reveals: Growth beyond coping

- Where am I still surviving instead of healing?
- What support helped me most?
- What am I ready to set down?

Wisdom to Carry Forward

- Divorce is an emotional earthquake, not a single event.
- Silence shapes children as much as words.
- Anger is often grief seeking safety.
- Survival skills protect—but healing frees.
- Not everything you carry belongs to you.
- Emotional literacy restores dignity.
- Understanding interrupts generational cycles.
- Your story can become wisdom instead of weight.

A GROUNDING WORD

"And now these three remain: faith, hope and love.
But the greatest of these is love."
—1 Corinthians 13:13

Closing Blessing

May you honor the child who didn't yet have language.
May you release what was never yours to carry.
May your story become wisdom, not weight.
And may dignity guide every relationship you
choose from here forward,
as you take your place again in the Ring—
wiser, softer, and whole.

Journey Fourteen

THE WISDOM OF OUR CAREERS

"If you don't feel it, flee from it.
Go where you are celebrated, not merely tolerated."
—Paul F. Davis

Where Work Lives in the Ring

EVERY RING OF WISDOM HAS A PLACE WHERE WE LEARN HOW WE CONTRIBUTE TO THE WORLD.

In this journey, that place is our work.

Not just the jobs we hold, but the way effort, excellence, belonging, worth, and identity quietly shape us over time. Our careers don't simply pay the bills; they teach us who we are allowed to be, how we are treated, and whether our gifts are welcomed or merely used.

This is the wisdom of our careers.

Finding Joy and Purpose in Work

I first learned about work ethic and the importance of loving what you do when I was seven years old.

Summers meant babysitters, which I dreaded. The days felt long and dull, and I craved movement, purpose, and adventure, not hours of sitting still.

Thankfully, I had another option: Saturdays at work with my mother or tagging along with my grandmother, Flora.

The choice was easy.

Going to work with my mother wasn't terrible, but it wasn't fun either. I took rollers out of women's hair, cleaned combs, folded towels. Occasionally I got to walk into town for a movie or a sweet treat from the bakery, but mostly it was routine.

Once, I blurted out that everyone's hair looked the same when they left.

My mother shushed me quickly.

Never say that to a customer.

That day I learned something important: For many women, the weekly wash, rollers, dry, and cloud of hairspray wasn't just about hair.

It was a way of connecting to other women.

It was ritual.

It was comfort.

It was feeling like themselves again.

Still...it wasn't for me.

What I dreamed about was becoming a stewardess. Stewardess is what they called a flight attendant back then. It sounded glamorous. A way out into the world.

Working with my grandmother, however, was something else entirely.

A Standard of Excellence

My grandmother worked as a chambermaid at a resort hotel in the Catskills, a place full of life, culture, and dignity.

The guests expected excellence, and she took immense pride in her work. Every room mattered. Every detail counted. She smiled at the guests, and they smiled right back.

Many asked about her winters and my grandfather, Howard, as if they were family. Their kindness extended to me, often telling me how wonderful my grandmother was and how lucky I was to have her.

I agreed completely.

I didn't just observe. I learned.

I could make a bed and clean a bathroom better than most kids my age. That attention to detail followed me home. My bedroom stayed neat except, of course, during my teenage years when outfits piled up on my bed before school.

But before bed, everything was folded or hung.

Order helped me rest.

Years later, I noticed the same trait in my daughter Liz—that same need for order, care, and completion.

Children are always watching.

They absorb our standards of excellence long before they choose their own careers.

Being Rewarded for Good Work

I also learned early that when you show up and do good work, one of two things happens:

You are rewarded.

Or you reward yourself by knowing you gave your best.

Sometimes that inner pride is enough.

And sometimes, the world responds.

My grandmother's rewards were simple and meaningful. A small yellow envelope with a few dollars. An ice cream cone on the way home. A swim in the hotel's indoor pool after her shift.

Ice cream and the pool became our ritual.

It wasn't just a treat.

It was acknowledgment.

Connection.

A shared celebration of effort.

Other days, hotel counselors invited me to join their groups of children while my grandmother finished her work. I felt welcomed. Valued. Included.

Those moments taught me something lasting:

When you do even the smallest job with care, people notice. And the reward isn't always money or praise.

Sometimes, it's being invited in.

The Warmth of Belonging

One of the most powerful lessons I learned was how the hotel staff treated my grandmother and how that treatment extended to me.

It felt like family.

The owners greeted her warmly. The baker invited me into the kitchen, sharing her craft, her attention, and her treats. I watched her knead dough and make desserts with tenderness and care.

That environment set my internal standard for work and how I hired people:

Would people take pride in what they do?

Would they treat others with respect?

Would generosity matter more than status?

From my grandparents and parents, I learned a simple, enduring formula:

Show up.

Take pride.

Support others.

Find joy in the work.

Grease, Groceries, and Growing Up

As I grew older, I explored many kinds of work: babysitting, caregiving, skating-rink shifts, and food service.

But the toughest job was working at my dad's service station.

I learned two things quickly:

I didn't want to smell like gas every day.

And hard labor matters.

I pumped gas, washed windshields, checked oil, and watched my dad work with precision and pride.

At sixteen, I worked at ShopRite. Then McDonald's, where I thrived on energy, pace, and people. A manager noticed my work ethic and offered me a higher-paying job at Burger King.

Here's what also became clear:

Better opportunities often come from doing good work.

But there's a hidden lesson in being excellent.

Sometimes your reliability becomes the reason you're kept in place—valuable, but overlooked for growth. The possibility that also occurs when you are loyal is that you can be taken advantage of.

Those early jobs shaped how I see work and leadership.

Hard work matters.

Curiosity matters.

And fit matters.

Choosing a Career Path

I didn't become a stewardess.

Instead, I followed in my mother's footsteps and became a hairdresser. At seventeen, it was a way to earn a living. I thought it would be temporary.

It wasn't.

Cosmetology wasn't about hair for me; it was about people. Helping someone walk out feeling seen, confident, and valued.

What began as a way to learn a skill while going to high school became a twenty-year career I loved.

In between my years of salon ownership, I had the opportunity to buy a bakery. My hometown bakery where I was a frequent buyer when I was a child.

It was exhausting, demanding, and stretching in ways nothing else had ever been. I built it with care. I honored it with long hours and deep commitment. And eventually, I let it go.

Even when something isn't meant to last forever, it still matters. What endured most from that season wasn't the business itself; it was the gift it gave my family.

Baking became a language of love in our home. Every year since my children were little, I've made the cake they ask for and the dinner they choose. Flour, frosting, and celebration became our tradition. One that carries memory, creativity, and love.

That chapter didn't end.

It transformed into something sweeter, shared, and lasting.

Once again, I leaned into what I knew I was good at, and this time, I was ready to expand my wings. I opened a spa and employed nine service providers. It felt like a dream realized: growth, leadership, contribution. A new place in the Ring where confidence and capability met opportunity.

And for a while, it worked.

Until it didn't.

Success came with a cost I hadn't realized. Long hours quietly replaced presence. Margin disappeared. My husband and I became like two ships passing—anchored to the same life, but rarely sharing the same moment.

One afternoon, sitting with my children after school, the Ring tightened around my heart. I could feel it—wisdom rising, asking to be listened to. I saw how quickly they were growing. My oldest, just twelve, was already stepping into pre-teen terrain that I knew required more than logistics or love in passing. It required presence. Bandwidth. Availability of heart and time.

And then the deeper truth surfaced: This wasn't just about one child or one year. This was the beginning of a new season for *all* of them.

I remembered my own teenage years, how both joyful and brutal they were. How friendships could lift you one day and break you the next. How confidence could disappear overnight. And now, layered into my children's lives, was a rapidly expanding digital world— more information, more comparison, more influence than any working parent could fully monitor from the sidelines.

The Ring of Wisdom doesn't ask us to abandon our gifts. It asks us to reprioritize them.

This wasn't a decision rooted in guilt or failure. It was rooted in discernment—the wisdom of knowing when a season has given all it can, and when another season is asking to be honored. I wasn't choosing *between* work and motherhood. I was choosing *how* to practice both with dignity.

Eventually, I sold the salon and spent the time with my children that they needed, and which I did too. I was able to get certifications to become a coach while they were at school. It was a risky step, because in those days "coaching" for business and life was new. That was a decision that changed my life. Not because it required less of me, but because it aligned me. It allowed me to stay in my gifts while widening my presence at home. The Ring expanded not by adding more, but by placing what mattered most back at the center. The journey of coaching I was able to take into my real estate career.

After moving to Maine, I became a real estate broker, which gave me flexibility, purpose, and another way to serve people through meaningful transitions.

My career has never been a straight line.

And I wouldn't change that.

Parenthood Is a Profession

Before anything else, I want to acknowledge stay-at-home parents. Your work matters.

I lived that role, and it is one of the hardest jobs there is—no breaks, no raises, no recognition.

To every parent doing invisible labor:

You are seen.

You matter.

And it's okay to step outside the role for a moment to offer yourself a name other than Mom. Giving you room to breathe, time to laugh and to love yourself for a day's work well done. After 5:00 p.m., my name becomes Lola.

She lives in the Ring too, reminding me that caregiving and self-care can coexist, and that wisdom includes knowing when to rest.

Giving myself permission to rest also gave me clarity. It helped me recognize that work, like caregiving, must align with the season of life you're in.

Corporate Life and Self-Employment

I've lived both.

Corporate life brings structure, stability, systems—and often, a clear path for leadership development. It taught me how organizations function, how decisions are made, and how consistency creates momentum. It also revealed something deeper and often overlooked: People don't show up to work only for the paycheck.

They show up for connection.

For recognition.

For belonging.

For the *atta-boys*, the teamwork, the shared wins, and the camaraderie that makes effort feel meaningful.

What has changed is the landscape itself.

The corporate world today is not the same one I worked in years ago. Hierarchies are less rigid. Longevity no longer guarantees advancement. Titles are earned differently. And leadership—*real leadership*—looks less like command and more like collaboration.

Each generation brings its own wisdom into the workplace:

- Baby Boomers value structure, face-to-face communication, and respect for hierarchy. Many seek flexibility later in their careers, appreciating hybrid or work-from-home options as they transition toward retirement.

- Generation X prizes independence, adaptability, and work-life balance. They thrive with autonomy and appreciate stability without micromanagement.

- Millennials (Gen Y) want meaningful work, clear growth paths, and consistent feedback. They value collaboration, purpose, and organizations that stand for something beyond profit.

- Generation Z values diversity, personalization, and individuality. As digital natives, they communicate quickly and directly, crave skill development, mentorship, and leadership that listens rather than dictates.

Despite these differences, one truth remains constant across every generation:

Everyone wants to be respected.

Everyone wants clear communication.

Everyone wants flexibility, though what flexibility looks like evolves with time, technology, and life stage.

Self-employment carries freedom and risk in the same breath. Moving from entrepreneur to purposeful leader requires a shift from constantly *doing* the work to *leading* the work. It asks you to build systems, delegate with trust, and invite others into the vision.

Every stage of business growth demands growth in you. A business will rarely outgrow the person leading it. When you expand your capacity, you invite financial growth, deeper accountability, and a quieter, more meaningful question: *What do I want to leave behind?*

At that point, work becomes more than income.

Legacy becomes part of the work.

If corporate life taught me discipline and systems, self-employment taught me resilience and discernment. It asked me to listen more closely to my energy, my values, my family, and the season I was in.

Neither path is better.

Both carry wisdom.

The Ring of Wisdom reminds us that alignment matters more than titles.

And that work, like life, must evolve if it is to remain sustainable, meaningful, and whole.

Wisdom Moment

Your work is not just how you make money.

It is how you practice dignity—

how you show up, serve, grow, and choose what matters.

When your work aligns with your values,

it becomes more than a job.

It becomes a life.

A Pause for Reflection

Pause here.

Let your career story rise—not just the titles,

but the moments that shaped you.

The people who saw you.

The seasons that stretched you.

The chapters that no longer fit.

Careers—Your Reflective Journey

1. Early Influences and Foundations

Feels like: Nostalgia, roots

Reveals: How early experiences shaped your beliefs about work and worth

- What early experiences formed my work ethic or sense of responsibility?

- Who modeled pride, excellence, or sacrifice in their work?

- What beliefs about effort, success, or value did I inherit?

2. Belonging, Recognition, and Dignity

Feels like: Safety, appreciation, or invisibility

Reveals: The role of culture and connection in meaningful work

- Where have I felt truly seen and valued in my career?
- Where have I felt overlooked or tolerated instead of celebrated?
- What does dignity look like in my work environment now?

3. When Reliability Becomes a Cage

Feels like: Pressure, restlessness, responsibility

Reveals: A season calling for advocacy or change

- How has my dependability served me—and limited me?
- What have I been carrying out of loyalty instead of alignment?
- What conversation or boundary would honor my growth?

4. Purpose, Pivot, and Legacy

Feels like: Courage, uncertainty, possibility

Reveals: Alignment between work, life, and meaning

- What season of work am I in right now?
- Where might I be invited to pivot or expand?
- What legacy do I want my work to leave—in my family, my community, and myself?

Wisdom to Carry Forward

- Early work experiences shape beliefs about effort and worth.
- Pride in your work is self-respect.
- Growth often requires pivots.
- Reliability is powerful—but should not become a cage.
- Coaching and mentorship accelerate clarity.
- Money is a tool, not meaning.
- Corporate life teaches structure; self-employment teaches resilience.
- Belonging matters in work cultures.

A GROUNDING WORD

"Whatever your hand finds to do, do it with your might."
—Ecclesiastes 9:10

Closing Blessing

May you honor the work you've done—seen and unseen.
May you release chapters that no longer fit.
May you be celebrated where you are,
and be brave enough to move when you're not.
And may your career support a life that feels honest,
meaningful, and true.

Journey Fifteen

THE WISDOM OF MONEY

*"The pursuit of money never ends when
you position it as a measure of happiness.
Instead, keep it as a tool to pursue what you love."*
—Adela Belin

Where Money Lives in the Ring

Money lives in the Ring as both mirror and messenger.

It reflects our values, our fears, our hopes, and our sense of safety.

It carries emotion long before it carries numbers.

The wisdom of money is not about accumulation.

It is about relationship.

It reveals how we relate to security, choice, control, and trust.

And like every relationship, money shows us where we feel grounded—and where we feel exposed.

This part of the Ring underpins how we dream, plan, and move through life.

It reminds us that while money itself does not create happiness, it does influence our sense of stability and our ability to shape our days.

There is a universal desire beneath our relationship with money:

to feel safe, to have agency, to make choices that reflect who we are becoming.

Money does not make us whole.

But when approached with wisdom, intention, and planning, it can support the life we are building—

and the dreams we are willing to believe in.

Ding Means Money

My emotional education around money began long before I knew the word *mindset*.

It started in my mother's salon on small-town Saturdays, sweeping hair, folding towels, earning a few dollars, and listening for the sound that made my heart leap: *Ding*.

That cash-register sound meant a sale.

It meant value exchanged.

It meant someone walked out feeling better because my mom had served them well.

I didn't know it then, but those Saturdays planted beliefs that still live in me:

- When you work, you earn.
- When you serve, people return.
- When money moves, dignity moves with it. My parents relentlessly worked hard—building cash-flow businesses where money moved in a steady rhythm. My dad carried a thick wad of bills in his pocket. My mom ran her salon with pride, precision, and grace.

From the outside, there was abundance.

Inside the home, there was tension.

Money wasn't talked about.

It was reacted to.

It wasn't about status.

It was about *safety*.

And safety, when threatened, carries emotion.

How Environment Shapes Money Beliefs

After my parents divorced, money became the center of everything between them.

My mother tried to preserve the life we knew.

My father tightened control.

Asking for money from my father for school clothes, shoes, or cleats felt humiliating.

Money came with conditions.

Ease disappeared.

That's when I learned something I couldn't name yet:

We inherit emotional money stories long before we ever earn a dollar.

I grew up in an environment where prosperity was visible—hotels buzzing, businesses thriving, money flowing. That taught me *there could be enough.*

But inside my home, I absorbed something else:

Fear.

Judgment.

Silence.

Scarcity.

Those stories followed me into adulthood, quietly shaping decisions, reactions, and expectations.

The Root of Money Is Emotional and Embodied

Money is not neutral.

It lives in the nervous system.

It can feel like:

- Safety or threat
- Freedom or confinement
- Worth or shame

We don't just manage money.

We manage what money *represents*.

Fear thinks short-term.

Wisdom thinks long-term.

And without emotional literacy, money decisions are often made from emotional saturation, not clarity.

When Money Is Misunderstood

Money is often taught as math, discipline, or restraint.

Rarely is it taught as emotional relationship.

When money becomes identity, shame follows.

When money becomes control, fear grows.

When money becomes silence, misunderstanding multiplies.

Money was never meant to carry the weight of our worth.

When the Money Flow Shifts

Years later, my husband Scott and I believed our finances were steady.

Pensions. Retirement accounts. Modest savings.

We weren't wealthy, but we felt secure.

Then came the real estate crash of 2009.

Business slowed. Bills stacked up. We sold things we loved. We borrowed. We drained retirement accounts that were meant to protect our future.

And then Scott lost his job.

Survival mode took over.

At the time, I didn't yet have emotional literacy. I didn't know how to name what was happening inside me. I only knew how to brace myself.

Our children felt it too.

They asked the question every parent dreads:

"Are we broke?"

I carried dignity the only way I knew how.

I worked. I adapted. I took a seasonal job not out of desire, but responsibility.

That season humbled me.

And it strengthened me.

Money may fall apart.

But you don't have to.

You rebuild.

You regulate.

You remember your worth.

What I understand now but didn't then is how essential it is to recognize the emotions money activates. I was experiencing all of them at once: intense anxiety, overwhelming fear, shame, guilt, and anger. The weight of it was impacting both my marriage and my mental health.

Thank goodness for children, because we didn't feel we had the luxury of collapsing. We didn't spend time analyzing how we felt. We just knew we had to get through it.

Still, the nights were hard.

I cried quietly for months.

Scott was my anchor—steady, calm, repeating, *"Everything is going to be okay."*

Another unexpected effect of that season was our lack of motivation to manage our finances at all. It felt pointless. The more we talked about it or even thought about it, the heavier everything became. Avoidance felt easier than facing the fear of our reality.

And yet, in the middle of that darkness, something beautiful emerged.

Community.

Family and friends showed up in ways we will never forget. My mother-in-law helped us pay our mortgage for months. Our dear friends Dennis and GG bought us a Christmas tree after our daughter mentioned we didn't have one.

Those gestures carried us.

One wisdom Scott and I will always hold close is the feeling of despair itself, because it taught us compassion we could never have learned any other way.

And here is another truth I want to name clearly:

We were grateful for the money we *had* saved. Those retirement accounts existed for a reason. A "rainy day" isn't always a drizzle; sometimes it's a downpour.

If you are holding funds and thinking, *I cannot touch that,* I invite you to also consider the emotional strain you may be carrying. You made money once. You can make it again. You will. What you gain in wisdom and resilience during hardship often becomes the very thing that rebuilds your future.

After that season, I spent a year reading about the psychology of money, learning how deeply fear, identity, and worth are intertwined with finances.

And here is what I want you to hear most clearly:

Reach out for help.

Do not be ashamed.

Listen to stories of people who lost everything—and came back. Some more than once.

A few you many know.

Steve Jobs, Ulysses S. Grant, Mark Twain, Martha Stewart, Dorothy Hamill, Walt Disney, George Foreman, Willie Nelson, Lady Gaga.

If they could rebuild, why not you?

Wisdom Moment

Money is a tool, not your worth.

The wisdom is in how you use it, grow it, and relate to it.

A Pause for Reflection

Money will always carry emotion.

But it never gets to define your value.

Before reflecting, pause and notice:

What does money feel like in your body right now?

Money—Your Reflective Journey

1. When You Feel Stable

Feels like: Calm, grounded, steady

Reveals: Your relationship with safety

- When have I felt most financially secure?
- What habits or choices created that steadiness?
- What does "enough" look like for me now?

2. When You Feel Stressed

Feels like: Pressure, overwhelm

Reveals: Fear of not enough

- What triggers my money anxiety?

- How do I react when money feels tight?

- What helps me regulate before deciding?

3. When Shame Shows Up

Feels like: Hiding, shrinking

Reveals: Old beliefs about worth

- Where did this money belief begin?

- Whose voice do I hear when shame appears?

- What would compassion sound like instead?

4. When You Feel Free

Feels like: Expansion, choice

Reveals: Alignment with values

- What does financial freedom mean to me?
- Where do I already experience freedom?
- What choices would support more of it?

Wisdom to Carry Forward

- Money is a tool—not your identity.
- Emotional literacy matters more than numbers.
- Fear shortens vision; wisdom widens it.
- Don't decide in the midst of emotional saturation.
- Adaptability protects dignity.
- Generosity recalibrates the spirit.
- Peace is real wealth.

A GROUNDING WORD

*"And my God will meet all your needs according
to the riches of his glory in Christ Jesus."*
—Philippians 4:19

Closing Blessing

May scarcity soften.
May shame loosen.
May dignity lead.
You are not defined by what you earn, spend, or save.
You are defined by the wisdom, intention, and heart behind it.
And in the Ring of Wisdom,
money takes its rightful place—
not as ruler,
but as servant.

Journey Sixteen

THE WISDOM OF COMMUNITY

*"The body is a community made up of its
innumerable cells or inhabitants."*
—Thomas Edison

Where Community Lives in the Ring

COMMUNITY LIVES IN THE RING AS CONNECTION—the fire of togetherness, surrounded by a circle of stones that both protect it and make space for vulnerability.

It is where joy is felt.

Where pain is seen and heard.

And like fire, community is not always gentle.

Sometimes it roars and consumes.

Sometimes it burns slowly, offering warmth to some while leaving others on the edge, unsure where they belong.

Community reflects who we are becoming through who we belong to. It teaches us how to show up, how to hold one another, and how to remain human through seasons of joy, fracture, and repair.

Long before I understood community as wisdom,

I was shaped by it.

A Living Tapestry of Connection

Community was one of my earliest teachers.

It formed my sense of identity long before I knew I was being shaped, and it taught belonging, empathy, resilience, and shared humanity.

Community is not defined by geography alone.

It is defined by people who show up. Who offer their stories, their presence, and the quiet wisdom of living connected rather than alone.

This is the wisdom that raised me.

The wisdom that met me in childhood, challenged me in adolescence, guided me into adulthood, and continues to ground me today.

Community is both soft and strong. One of the greatest realities we will ever know, and one of the clearest mirrors for who we are becoming.

A Community Woven in Wisdom

I grew up in Livingston Manor, New York, a small hamlet in the Catskill Mountains. My first true community, nestled in a quiet valley that felt both safe and expansive. The sound of the Willowemoc Creek was the heartbeat of our town. A beautiful brick school built in 1939 stood proudly at its center.

A stone bridge connected us to Main Street, where neighbors waved, horns offered friendly greetings, and afternoons echoed with laughter as kids gathered after school.

There were restaurants, bars, owner-operated hotels, small shops, and two grocery stores, three churches, and a synagogue. All this served around 4,000 people. The real wealth of our community wasn't in its businesses.

It was in how people cared for one another.

I could wander mountains, railroad tracks, and quiet roads knowing I was held within an invisible web of connection. You didn't have to know everyone personally. Knowing *of* them was often enough.

Safety lived in that closeness.

Belonging had a pulse.

How Community Shows Up Across Seasons

Our town wasn't just a dot on the map. It stretched across winding roads, connecting neighboring hamlets—each with its own character.

One was known for grand hotels and covered bridges.

Another for hunting and fishing shops and antiques.

Another for a diner that felt like home.

Another for lakes that invited stillness.

Each place held its own kind of magic.

At the time, it was simply home.

Looking back, I see how rare it was.

Learning from Community

Although small, Livingston Manor held meaningful diversity of cultures, languages, foods, traditions, and stories that enriched our collective life. As a child, I didn't categorize people by difference. I understood them through connection. When you know someone personally, labels soften. I heard narrow-minded comments from time to time, beliefs passed down like a worn coat, but I rarely saw true hate.

What I saw most often was decency.

Neighbors helping neighbors.

Families sharing food.

Kids playing side by side.

Those seeds became part of my core—empathy, kindness, and the ability to see people beyond labels. But as I grew, I learned something else too:

Community doesn't only reveal our capacity for connection. It also reveals our capacity for judgment.

What once felt like belonging can, over time, begin to feel like scrutiny.

The same closeness that holds you can also watch you.

And that is where community begins to change.

When Community Becomes Complicated

As I grew older, the closeness that once felt comforting sometimes felt confining. In a town where everyone knows everyone, mistakes don't stay quiet.

Bullying entered my world.

My parents' divorce added emotional weight.

High school became a landscape of shifting identity and expectations.

The town changed too; jobs faded, businesses and hotels were closing, and stability slipped.

Yet anchors remained:

- youth ministers who listened
- friends who accepted me
- nature that welcomed me without question
- community gatherings that kept us stitched together

We didn't always name what was hard.

But we endured together.

Shared struggle builds resilience.

That is what community does.

Leaving—and Returning

By graduation, I felt torn—rooted in what was familiar, yet quietly called toward something new. Leaving wasn't dramatic. It happened in gentle increments: packed boxes, long hugs, and a hesitant goodbye. I headed to Florida believing a new beginning was possible.

And in many ways, it was.

I built a life there filled with energy, opportunity, and motion. Everything moved faster. People moved faster. Money flowed more openly. Towering homes overlooked the ocean and the Intracoastal, shimmering with possibility. It was exciting. It was busy. It was nothing like my one-horse town, as people would refer to it.

My small-town ways, though, didn't quite fit. People didn't slow down. Eye contact was rare. Conversations felt transactional instead of relational. Still, I was fascinated. I learned. I grew. I stretched.

Florida brought wonder and it brought lessons.

It was also where life delivered some of its hardest knocks. When my marriage ended there, far from family and the quiet security of home, the loneliness was devastating. Without the familiar net of community beneath me, I felt untethered, learning in real time how much belonging matters when life begins to unravel.

After my divorce, I returned home. A place where I felt I could find solace again.

Looking back, I see the wisdom in that return. Had I not gone back, I would never have met my husband.

What felt like a step backward became a doorway forward.

Finding Home Again

Fourteen years later into our marriage, Maine called us home.

I had been to Maine when I was five years old and then summers for 14 years with our children at our cottage, and something about the move felt safe. Something about this move felt like I was coming home. It felt safe and nourishing. I remembered the loon songs on the lake at my uncle's home, the salt air at the pier and ocean, and the quiet power that seemed to be in the energy of people.

Florida gave me opportunity. New York gave me love and family. Maine gave me peace.

And Livingston Manor will always remain in my heart.

Belonging, I learned, isn't tied to geography.

It's tied to how we show up.

The Root of Community

Community offers what you offer it.

Bring warmth—and you'll find warmth.

Bring openness—and connection will meet you there.

Show up with kindness—and it will be reflected back to you.

Community is not built by perfection.

It is built by presence—by staying engaged as it grows, shifts, and evolves.

True community requires courage and vision: the willingness to hold both similarities *and* differences with curiosity.

It asks us to listen instead of assume.

To repair instead of retreat.

To include instead of exclude.

To remain even when it feels uncomfortable.

Diversity deepens wisdom when dignity leads.

And yet, our world today feels more divided than ever. The volume of concern has grown loud. It appears that leaders in our communities are being led by fear rather than kindness, suspicion rather than compassion. Fear of our neighbor fractures what was meant to connect us.

Now more than ever, community matters.

Now more than ever, we must reach out.

Ask someone how they are *and mean it.*

Those who live in fear are often the quietest.

Community begins when someone notices and chooses to care.

Wisdom Moment

Community is not built by perfection. It is built by presence and love. Strength and courage.

A Pause for Reflection

As you decide on your next journey of wisdom, notice where you feel held and where you long to belong. Community is not something you find once. It is something you feel and care about, that aligns with your values.

Community—Your Reflective Journey

1. When You Feel Belonging

Feels like: Safety, inclusion

Reveals: Your need to be seen and accepted

- Where do I feel most at home?
- How do I help others feel they belong?
- What allows me to soften and be myself in community?

2. When Community Is Tested

Feels like: Discomfort, courage

Reveals: Growth through difference and repair

- How do I respond to conflict or difference?
- What repair might be needed—by me or with others?
- Where am I being invited to stay present instead of pulling away?

3. When You Contribute

Feels like: Purpose, impact

Reveals: Everyone has something to offer

- What do I naturally bring to my community?
- Where am I being called to serve or show up more fully?
- How does my presence affect the spaces I enter?

4. When You Consider Legacy

Feels like: Reflection, meaning

Reveals: The imprint you leave behind

- What do I want to be remembered for in my community?

- What values do I want others to feel when they are with me?

- What small act today could shape that legacy in the future?

Wisdom to Carry Forward

- Community shapes identity and belonging.
- Shared struggle builds resilience.
- Connection dissolves labels.
- Presence strengthens bonds.
- Diversity deepens wisdom.
- Dignity sustains belonging.
- Community reflects how we show up.
- Legacy is formed through consistent care.

A GROUNDING WORD

"And let us consider how we may spur one another on toward love and good deeds, not giving up meeting together,… but encouraging one another."
—Hebrews 10:24–25

Closing Blessing

May your community connect, heal, and hold you.
May you notice where doors are opening—and where you are
invited to step forward.
You were never meant to do life alone.
Carry what resonated.
And let the wisdom of community walk with you—
into the next conversation,
the next gathering,
the next chapter.

Journey Seventeen

THE WISDOM OF GRIEF

*"You can't truly heal from a loss until you
allow yourself to really feel the loss."*
—Mandy Hale

Where Grief Lives in the Ring

GRIEF LIVES IN THE RING AS A THRESHOLD.

It marks the place where love meets loss, where something meaningful has changed forever.

Grief is not the fire itself; it is the ache left behind when the fire shifts or goes out.

It circles what mattered.

It guards what was sacred.

And it asks us to slow down enough to feel what we would rather outrun.

Before I understood grief as wisdom, I only knew it as pain.

Now I know it as a teacher. Quiet, relentless, and profoundly human.

When Grief Walked Beside Me

As I was finishing the final chapters of this book, grief sat down beside me.

One of my dear friends was dying of cancer.

From diagnosis to her passing was just over a year, and even now, it doesn't feel real. Watching someone you love wither, watching their light dim and then gently go out is a kind of suffering that rearranges you. There was nothing dramatic about it. Just a slow, devastating awareness that time was running out.

She left behind a three-year-old child, a husband, and a new home still being built. She fought fiercely. She prayed faithfully. She loved Jesus deeply right to the very end.

Whatever the plan was, it was not one I would have chosen.
And yet, grief did not ask my permission to arrive.

What Grief Really Is (And Isn't)

Grief has no boundaries.

No straight line.

No predictable direction.

It shows up like an uninvited companion—persistent, inconvenient, impossible to ignore. Some days it hums quietly in the background. Other days it overwhelms the nervous system, heavy and unrelenting.

Grief is not only about death. It is about *loss*—any loss that matters.

I have known grief many times:

- grief in my parents' divorce
- grief in my own divorce
- grief in giving up breastfeeding
- grief watching my first child walk into school
- grief closing a business that held my heart
- grief losing financial security
- grief parenting a child with special needs
- grief watching someone lose dignity through illness
- grief sending a child off to college

Grief does not discriminate.

If you have loved, you will grieve.

Grief in the Body and the Emotional World

Grief is not just emotional; it is *somatic*. The body holds it with reverence.

Heaviness in the chest.

Fatigue that sleep doesn't fix.

A fog that dulls color and sound.

And the emotions; oh, the emotions:

Sadness.

Despair.

Anguish.

Loneliness.

Guilt.

Anger.

These emotions are not problems to solve. They are signals asking for tenderness

And yet this is often when we are hardest on ourselves. We show up beautifully for others who grieve. Meals. Messages. Flowers. Presence.

But when it is our turn?

We rush. We minimize. We judge. We ask, *Why am I still not okay?*

When Grief Is Misunderstood

We are told there are stages of grief—five, seven, maybe more.

Denial.

Anger.

Bargaining.

Depression.

Acceptance.

Loneliness.

Reflection.

Recovery.

But grief does not move in order.

These are not steps to complete.

They are emotions arriving to support us, even when they feel unbearable.

Grief doesn't mean something is wrong with you. It means something mattered.

What Grief Teaches

Grief brings life into focus.

It strips away what is trivial.

It clarifies what matters.

It deepens empathy.

It matures the heart.

Grief does not erase joy, but it changes it.

Joy becomes quieter. More honest. Less performative.

And slowly, if we allow it, grief expands us.

Not by forgetting.

But by integrating.

Wisdom Moment

Grief opens the heart in ways we never expect.

The wisdom is in trusting that love does not end—it transforms.

A Pause for Reflection

You do not have to rush this. You do not have to be strong today.

Take a breath. Notice what you've lost.

Notice what you're still carrying.

This is not about "getting over" anything.

It is about walking with what has happened.

Grief—Your Reflective Journey

1. When Loss First Arrived

Feels like: Shock, disbelief, numbness

Reveals: Something meaningful has changed

- What loss am I still trying to understand?

- What did that loss take from me?

- What part of me needs gentleness right now?

2. When the Weight Settles In

Feels like: Heaviness, fatigue, fog

Reveals: Grief lives in the body, not just the mind

- Where do I feel grief in my body?
- What does my body need instead of pressure?
- How can I offer myself rest without guilt?

3. When Emotions Feel Too Much

Feels like: Anger, guilt, despair, overwhelm

Reveals: Emotions asking to be honored, not avoided

- Which emotion have I been resisting most?
- What might it be trying to protect or reveal?
- What would compassion sound like toward myself?

4. When Meaning Begins to Shift

Feels like: Perspective, tenderness, quiet strength

Reveals: Growth does not erase loss—it lives beside it

- What has grief clarified about what matters?
- How has this loss changed me?
- What wisdom do I want to carry forward?

Wisdom to Carry Forward

- Grief is the cost of love—and love is worth it.
- There is no timeline for healing.
- Emotions are messengers, not failures.
- The body needs compassion as much as the heart.
- You do not need to grieve alone.
- Meaning can grow alongside sorrow.
- You are not broken—you are becoming.

A GROUNDING WORD

"The Lord is close to the brokenhearted and saves
those who are crushed in spirit."
—Psalm 34:18

Closing Blessing

May you allow grief its voice—without judgment.
May you rest when your body asks.
May you accept support when strength feels thin.
May you remember:
You are not failing because you feel deeply.
You are human.
And may the Ring hold your sorrow gently—
not to trap it,
but to honor it
as part of the wisdom you now carry forward.

Journey Eighteen

THE WISDOM OF SPIRITUALITY

"Our breath is the bridge from our body to our mind."
—Thich Nhat Hanh

Where Spirituality Lives in the Ring

Spirituality lives in the Ring as bond of the unseen thread that binds body, mind, heart, and meaning.

It is the quiet fire at the center: not loud, not forced, not performative, but steady, sustaining, and alive.

Spirituality reflects how we relate to what we cannot control, how we find meaning when answers are thin, and how we remain human through joy, suffering, doubt, and dignity.

Before I understood spirituality as wisdom, I only knew it as *something bigger than me*—a presence, a current of energy unlike anything I could name or control.

It felt expansive and mysterious.

An openness to the unknown.

A quiet awareness that life held more than what I could see or explain.

That early sense of *something more* shaped how I approached spirituality long before I had language for it. And yet, naming spirituality aloud is often where things tighten in a group.

A Quiet Conversation About Spirituality

The moment spirituality is mentioned, people often brace themselves, unsure of where the conversation might lead. For some, the word carries judgment or rigidity.

For others, comfort, curiosity, or home.

Yet across cultures and generations, the longing is the same: strength when life is heavy, hope when the path is unclear,

meaning beyond what we can touch.

For me, spirituality shows up as *God winks*—

small moments of clarity, comfort, or quiet assurance

that remind me I am seen and not walking alone.

My faith is anchored in God. However, I do not believe in forced belief.

What matters most to me is *how we show up*:

with kindness, honesty, compassion, and alignment.

That is spirituality lived.

My Spiritual Story

Growing up, I loved the stories of Jesus shared in church, music, and quiet moments at my grandmother Helena's kitchen table. Listening to 8-track tapes of Christian songs.

She shaped my faith more than any sermon.

She baked for people in need.

She welcomed everyone warmly.

And when my grandfather grumbled, she would say,

"You don't know their story. People come into our lives to teach us something."

Through her, I learned this truth:

Kindness is not optional; it is essential.

To love people as Jesus did.

Nothing more. Nothing less.

The Root of Spirituality

Like many of us, I inherited beliefs that mixed faith with fear:

Be good or else.

Bad things happen for a reason.

Questioning means failing.

Those beliefs shaped my early moral compass—

and also my anxiety.

Even now, when something goes wrong,

I can feel the old question arise:

What did I do wrong?

My faith gently rewrote that story.

I learned this slowly:

spirituality does not erase pain—

but it can become a place of healing.

Spiritual Myths I Had to Unlearn

- God is waiting for me to mess up → God is waiting for me to come home
- Spirituality requires perfection → It requires honesty and it's messy
- Questioning faith means losing it → It often deepens it
- Hard things mean punishment → They mean life is happening
- Love must be earned → Grace is received
- God lives only in church → God is everywhere

Letting go of these softened my faith and rooted it in love instead of fear. You learn faith by deciding what you'll chase for freedom to be your best self.

A Child Wandering Without Spirituality

After my parents' divorce, I drifted. I chased freedom and rebellion. I was angry at God. I wondered, *Does he really love me? What have I done to make this happen?* My spirituality compass's guidance was off course. My parents drifted from church, and there was nothing grounding in life anymore. What was there was a sense of something that was bigger than me, with no understanding of the faith that it would take to allow it.

But the inner voice planted in childhood never left me.

My return was not dramatic.

It was quiet.

Honest.

Hopeful and grace-filled.

One night, lying in the dark, I whispered:

"God...do You still see me?"

What followed was not spectacle—

just warmth.

A knowing.

A presence.

Yes. Always.

Spirituality in the Landscape

Nature has always been part of my spiritual language.

Rivers remind me to allow life to flow rather than resist it. Covered bridges stir a sense of nostalgia and history that grounds me, whispers of those who crossed before me and the paths that still hold us.

And then there are sunsets—my favorite teachers. The sky paints itself in endless colors, never repeating the same design twice. Each one reminds me that spirituality, like people, is not meant to look the same. Its beauty lives in its uniqueness.

On my walks, what I see and hear gently settles me. Nature wraps me in a quiet embrace offering peace, safety, and a steady strength that asks nothing from me except presence.

I always feel the same truth: There is something bigger than me.

That truth still grounds me even in the midst of life's unknown navigation.

But not everyone's experience with spirituality has felt grounding.

For many, spirituality was introduced through rules instead of relationship. Fear instead of freedom, and judgment instead of curiosity. What was meant to connect us instead created distance. What was meant to steady us sometimes became something to perform, prove, or obey. It's your faith that defines you.

And that is where misunderstanding begins.

When Spirituality Is Misunderstood

Spirituality is often mistaken for control, certainty, or compliance.

In truth, it is about deepening one's connection to self, cultivating inner peace, and fully embracing the human experience.

True spirituality invites inward growth and authenticity. It teaches us how to navigate daily life with presence rather than striving for perfection. It is not about escaping the physical world, but about living within it more consciously, compassionately, and awake.

Key misconceptions about spirituality include:

- Spirituality means always being positive.

  Spirituality is not the denial of anger, grief, or doubt. It is not a requirement to "stay high vibe" or avoid discomfort. Avoiding hard emotions does not make us enlightened—it makes us disconnected. True spirituality increases our capacity to feel deeply without being ruled by what we feel.

- Spirituality is the same as religion.

  While religion can be a pathway to spiritual growth, spirituality itself is not confined to doctrine, ritual, or institution. It is an inner awakening. A relationship with conscience. A practice of alignment. Some express it through faith traditions. Others express it through reflection, service, and intentional living. The essence is connection, not conformity.

- Spirituality means certainty.

  Many believe that spiritual maturity removes doubt. In reality, doubt often refines faith. Questions deepen understanding. Seasons of silence strengthen trust. Spiritual growth is not the absence of uncertainty. It is the courage to remain open within it.

- Spirituality means avoiding conflict.

  Spirituality is not passive. It does not require silence in the face of injustice or self-betrayal. True spirituality strengthens our backbone. It allows us to speak truth with dignity and set boundaries with compassion. Peace is not the same as compliance.

- Spirituality is separate from daily life.
  Spirituality is not reserved for Sunday mornings, meditation cushions, or retreats. It is revealed in how we respond under pressure, how we treat those who disagree with us, how we repair when we cause harm, and how we regulate when emotions rise. Spirituality is not escape from life. It is embodied within it.

- Spirituality is self-focused.
  While inner growth is essential, spirituality is not self-absorption. It expands us outward—toward service, contribution, and responsibility. It asks not only "How do I feel?" but also "How do I impact others?"

What I feel most important about spirituality is

It listens to me.

It helps me breathe more fully and expand into love.

It holds tension without rushing to resolve it.

It strengthens us not by removing hardship, but by giving us something steady to hold.

Spirituality became less about appearing good and more about becoming whole.

Wisdom Moment

Spirituality is your connection to God, to self, and to something greater.

The wisdom is in trusting the path, even when you cannot see it.

A Pause for Reflection

Before reflecting: Know that no matter what, you are loved,
and there is something bigger than you that has your back.

Your belief in what you believe about spirituality is more important than who knows about it and how it fills your soul.

Notice your breath.

Notice what softened as you read.

Notice what stirred resistance.

This is not about belief systems.

It is about you and your belief and your compass of
faith to guide you in living your best life.

Spirituality—Your Reflective Journey

1. When You Feel Connected

Feels like: Belonging, alignment

Reveals: A longing for meaning beyond self

- Where do I feel most spiritually connected?

- What practices help me return there?

- What part of me wants reconnection now?

2. When You Feel Present

Feels like: Stillness, grounded breath

Reveals: Wisdom lives in the now

- What pulls me out of presence most easily?
- What helps me return to my body and breath?
- What becomes available when I slow down?

3. When You Feel Compassion

Feels like: Softness, openness

Reveals: Love without conditions

- Where do I need to extend more grace?
- What story keeps my heart guarded?
- What would love do here?

4. When You Feel Surrender

Feels like: Peace, release

Reveals: Trust without certainty

- What am I trying to control?
- What might change if I loosened my grip?
- What is one next step I can trust?

Wisdom to Carry Forward

- Spirituality is relationship, not performance
- Grace meets us where we are
- Questions deepen wisdom
- Kindness is lived faith
- Presence is sacred
- You are never walking alone

A GROUNDING WORD

"Trust in the Lord with all your heart…"
—Proverbs 3:5

Closing Blessing

May your spirituality feel spacious, not heavy.
May curiosity replace fear.
May grace quiet perfection.
May you feel God in your breath,
in a kind word,
in the steady comfort of being held.
And may you remember—
you are seen, guided, and deeply loved.

Journey Nineteen

THE WISDOM OF BECOMING

"Wisdom does not shout. It settles."
—A Buddhist monk's philosophy

You've Been Walking This Longer Than You Think

IF YOU'RE HERE, SOMETHING HAS ALREADY SHIFTED.

Not because you rushed through the pages.

Not because you "figured anything out."

But because you stayed.

You stayed with the stories that stirred something tender.

You stayed with the memories that surfaced quietly.

You stayed with the questions that didn't demand answers right away.

That is how wisdom works.

It doesn't arrive with fireworks.

It arrives like breath. Steady, grounding, faithful.

This book was never meant to change you.

It was meant to remind you of who you already are.

The Ring Was Always Within You

Each journey you've walked from dignity, family, divorce, career, money, community, and spirituality is not a separate lesson.

They are rings of wisdom that help you become your best self. Living a thriving life.

Layered experiences. Intersecting truths and stories that circle back on one another.

That is the nature of wisdom.

It doesn't move in straight lines.

It spirals.

What you learned about dignity in one chapter may have echoed in another.

What surfaced in grief may have softened in forgiveness.

What once felt heavy may now feel lighter—not gone, but integrated.

The ring doesn't close because everything is resolved.

It closes because you are more whole.

What You Carry Forward

You may not remember every story.

You may not revisit every reflection.

My hope is that you will carry the *love* of this journey.

- A deeper respect for your emotional life
- A gentler relationship with your past
- A clearer sense of what belongs to you and what does not
- A steadier connection to dignity as your anchor
- A quieter confidence in how you show up

Wisdom doesn't ask you to be perfect.

It asks you to be present.

Living the Wisdom

This is where the book releases you—not away from it, but into your life.

Into conversations that require courage.

Into choices that reflect your values.

Into pauses where listening matters more than fixing.
Into relationships where dignity becomes a daily practice.
You don't need to teach this wisdom.
You live it.
In how you respond instead of react.
In how you hold boundaries with compassion.
In how you forgive without abandoning yourself.
In how you choose love again and again.
That is legacy.

When You Forget (Because You Will)

There will be days when you forget everything you've read.
Days when old patterns return.
Days when fear speaks louder than trust.
Days when you feel small again.
That doesn't mean the wisdom is gone.
It means you're human.
When that happens, come back to one simple truth:
Dignity never leaves you.
It waits patiently—for your breath, your pause, your return.

A GROUNDING WORD

*"Do not be conformed to this world, but be transformed by
the renewal of your mind, that by testing you may discern what
is the will of God, what is good and acceptable and perfect."*
—Romans 12:2

Closing Blessing

May you trust the wisdom you've earned.
May you honor the life that shaped it.
May you release what no longer needs to be carried.
May dignity guide your words, your choices, and your relationships.
May courage rise when it's needed.
May forgiveness soften what fear once hardened.
And may you remember always.
You are not becoming wise.
You already are.
You are simply learning to live it.

Journey Twenty

A COMPANION INVITATION

IF THIS JOURNEY HAS SPOKEN TO YOUR HEART, I've created a place
for you to continue the experience at www.theringofwisdom.com.
There, you'll find:

- A free, downloadable companion journal with guided prompts
  for deeper reflection

- An assessment designed to strengthen your emotional literacy and support ironclad connections
- A community rooted in growth, connection, and shared wisdom

This is not something you must complete.

It is simply an invitation.

You get to decide when the time feels right.

Wisdom honors timing.

If and when you feel called, you are welcome to join me there.

Until then, know this:

The most important work has already begun within you.

The circle is always open.

Closing the Circle

As you reach the end of this book, I hope you recognize something important: Wisdom was never meant to live only in these pages.

Wisdom is formed in quiet moments of reflection, in the emotions we learn to understand, in the courage it takes to grow, and in the stories we are brave enough to share. It is shaped through the relationships that support us, the challenges that stretch us, and the experiences that slowly reveal who we are becoming.

Often, wisdom is born through moments we did not ask for—through disappointment, pain, and sadness. Through the seasons of life that test our strength and invite us to look deeper within ourselves. Even in those moments, something meaningful is being formed.

Writing *The Ring of Wisdom* has been a deeply personal journey for me. Every chapter reflects moments of my own life—times of joy, uncertainty, growth, pain, and discovery. In sharing these stories, my hope has never been to suggest that I have all the answers, but rather to remind you that the wisdom you seek has always been forming within you as well.

Each of us carries our own ring of wisdom—built from the people who have shaped us, the lessons life has offered, and the choices we continue to make. Sometimes we recognize it clearly.

Other times, it takes reflection and patience to see the meaning within our experiences.

What matters most is that we stay curious about our lives.

We ask deeper questions.

We listen to our emotions rather than silence them.

We allow ourselves the courage to grow.

And perhaps most importantly, we give ourselves compassion for what we have been through. When we do, something powerful begins to happen. The weight we have carried softens, and we create space for bold, deep healing to begin.

Wisdom is not something we arrive at once. It is something we return to—again and again—as we continue learning, loving, and living.

If there is one hope I carry for you as you close this book, it is this: that you trust the wisdom already unfolding within your own life.

Your experiences matter.

Your story matters.

Even the chapters filled with uncertainty, grief, or struggle have something to teach.

And your dreams are worthy of being pursued.

It is never too late to pause and ask yourself a powerful question:

Why not me?

Why not live with greater intention?

Why not pursue the dreams that have been quietly waiting within your heart?

Why not step into the boldness of becoming who you were meant to be?

The journey of wisdom does not end here. In many ways, it is just beginning.

And wherever your path leads next, may you walk it with courage, reflection, and love.

Perhaps, somewhere along your journey, you will pause and notice something beautiful:

The wisdom was forming all along.

May your wisdom deepen, your dignity remain steady, and your life unfold with the boldness of a heart that finally trusts itself.

With much appreciation,

Sandy Bonney

Acknowledgments

WRITING THIS BOOK BEGAN AS A LEGACY PIECE FOR MY CHILDREN—something that could hold them when I am no longer physically present to listen, guide, or embrace them. A place they could return to when life feels uncertain. Small reminders of how life's moments—both tender and difficult—shape us into wiser, more compassionate humans. An invitation to pause, reflect, feel, and choose response over reaction. To live their best life with dignity, courage, and heart.

This book is dedicated to my children, my family, and the friends who have moved in and out of my life—those who stayed, those who shaped me for a season, and those whose love left a lasting imprint.

With deepest gratitude to my grandmothers, Helena Woehrle and Flora Lindsley.

I love and miss you both dearly. Your strength, steadiness, and unwavering love taught me what it truly means to care for family. You never spoke ill of anyone. You showed me—through example—that everyone matters and that every person carries a story of both pain and hope. Your wisdom lives on in me.

This book is also dedicated to the many women in my life who transformed me and loved me unconditionally. You helped shape my becoming more than you may ever know.

To my husband, who carried us financially during the last two years so I could have the space to discover myself more fully and bring this book into the world. Thank you for believing in me and for being my rock. Your support gave me the courage to keep going when the path felt uncertain.

To my four children, Christian, Liz, Brian, and Alicia. Thank you for being part of this book and part of my becoming. You are my greatest teachers, my deepest inspiration, and the reason so much of this wisdom lives within these pages. I love you more than words can hold.

To my mother, Joyce, who continues to model resilience, perseverance, and love well into her eighties. Your strength has been a quiet compass throughout my life.

To my childhood neighbor who became one of my dearest friends, Gail Lenkiewicz.

You exemplified what motherhood looks like—and how it grows and deepens over time. You and your husband, Tony, showed me that marriage takes work, love, patience, and commitment. You also showed me the power of family traditions—how they anchor a family and live on in the hearts of generations.

To my granddaughter, Lottie Elizabeth Leighton, whose joyful spirit and radiant smile melt my heart every time I am with you. You are a living reminder of hope, legacy, and love unfolding forward.

Special thanks to **my daughter-in-law Cheyenne Bonney** for her beautiful illustrations throughout the book.

To my dear friend, Kattie Hartwell, who left this world far too soon—cancer stole you too early. You were light and love in human form. I will never forget how gently you nudged me to keep going, even when I felt tired or unsure.

To my aunts, Margaret and Andrea. Thank you for always asking how the book was coming—especially when I needed encouragement most.

To my coach, Dan Newby, for teaching me emotional literacy, agility, regulation, and resilience—and for helping me see that being a visionary is not only important, but necessary.

And to Bethany, my writing coach and Publishing Partner, who was my lighthouse when I felt lost in the fog of despair and self-doubt. You helped me learn how to write, how to trust my voice, and how to believe that I am a writer—and that I could become an author. My heartfelt gratitude for every year you supported and guided me.

This book exists because of love, courage, faith, and the wisdom shared—spoken and unspoken—by those who walked beside me.

With love and gratitude,

Sandy

About the Author

SANDY BONNEY IS AN AUTHOR, LEADERSHIP COACH, SPEAKER, real estate broker, and Dignity Inc. Practitioner. With more than two decades of experience in real estate leadership, coaching, and training, she brings thought-provoking conversations to leaders, entrepreneurs, and professionals. Her work centers on a simple yet powerful belief: Sustainable success in business—and the ability to truly enjoy healthy, meaningful lives—begins with our willingness to acknowledge and navigate our emotions. Through her work in emotional literacy, dignity-based leadership, and reflective coaching, Sandy equips individuals and organizations to lead with greater dignity, passion, resilience, and authentic human connection.

Sandy lives a philosophy—Reconnect. Reframe. Rise. This philosophy grew from lived experience navigating love, loss, marriage, motherhood, business, and reinvention. She understands how easy it is to become consumed by achievement while losing touch with oneself, and how transformative it can be to reclaim presence, peace, courage, and dignity.

As a speaker and facilitator, Sandy brings inspiration, candor, and grounded insight to audiences navigating personal and professional transitions. Her work blends practical business wisdom with emotional insight, inviting people to step into their boldness—not reck-lessly, but with the steady courage that comes from understanding what works best for them. She reminds leaders and individuals alike that emotional awareness and regulation is not a soft skill; it is the foundational skill.

Sandy lives in Maine with her husband and pup Ella. She is the proud mother of four children and grandmother to Lottie. Surrounded by family and the natural beauty of New England, you'll often find her either on an island or in the mountains. For Sandy, time in nature offers the kind of stillness that invites reflection.